While In The Storm

Devotionals and Prayers when Facing
Transition, Trials, and Temptations

Edward O. Anderson, Jr.

"Be still, and know that I am God."
- Psalm 46:10

While In
The Storm

Devotionals and Prayers when Facing
Transition, Trials, and Temptations

Edward O. Anderson, Jr.

Future of Hope Ministries Publishing
Phoenix, Arizona

"He will keep in perfect peace those whose minds are steadfast."
- Isaiah 26:3

While in the Storm: Devotionals and Prayers for Life's Transitions, Trials, and Temptations
First Edition • Printed in the United States of America

ISBNs
Paperback: 978-1-970836-00-4
Hardcover: 978-1-970836-02-8
eBook: 978-1-970836-01-1

Scripture Credits
Scripture quotations are taken from the following translations:
• New King James Version (NKJV) © 1982 by Thomas Nelson, Inc. Used by permission. All rights reserved.
• King James Version (KJV) Public Domain.
• Revised Standard Version (RSV) © 1946, 1952 by the Division of Christian Education of the National Council of the Churches of Christ in the U.S.A. Used by permission. All rights reserved.

Cover Design and Interior Layout: Edward O. Anderson, Jr., Future of Hope Creative Designs
Published by: Future of Hope Publishing
Phoenix, Arizona   •   FutureOfHope.com

For information regarding bulk purchases, ministry distribution, or media rights, please contact:
FutureOfHope.com
Info@FutureOfHope.com

Printed and distributed through Amazon KDP and IngramSpark under license. eBook and Audiobook produced and distributed by Future of Hope Ministries.

Library of Congress Control Number: Pending

Illustrations, Images & Design Notice

Public Figures & Story Disclaimer

"We tell stories not to glorify people,
but to magnify the God who redeems them."
— Pastor Ed Anderson

Dedication

To all who have heard the gentle call of the Holy Spirit
and have stepped boldly into the waters of baptism—

To those who have rededicated their hearts through rebaptism,
renewing their covenant with the Savior—

To those who have chosen to go all in for God,
leaving behind the lukewarm comfort of Laodicea
for the refining fire of wholehearted devotion—

And to all who continue steadfastly on their spiritual journeys,
drawing closer to God even while under the attacks of the enemy—

This book is dedicated to you.
May your faith hold firm in the storm,
your heart remain tender to His voice,
and your life reflect the steadfast love of the One
who still speaks, "Peace, be still."

Acknowledgments

My heart is filled with gratitude to everyone who helped bring *While in the Storm* to life.

To my wife Angela and our family—thank you for your patience, prayers, and love through each season of ministry. To my children, whose joy reminds me daily that God still speaks peace into the chaos—thank you for believing in this mission.

To my *Arizona Conference* family and Pastoral friends and colleagues, church family, ministry teams, elders, deacons, translators, musicians, and mission supporters—you are my partners in hope.

To those who prayed, donated, traveled, and labored with us on the front lines of evangelism—this book carries your fingerprints of faith.

And above all, to my Lord and Savior Jesus Christ—thank You for the storms that shape us, the grace that sustains us, and the peace that passes understanding.

All glory and honor to God, who still calms the storm.

TABLE OF CONTENTS

Day 40 - When God Wipes Every Tear.....203

Introduction - Why 40 Days?

This book is about spiritual focus.

When a person experiences spiritual growth, personal transition, temptation, a great trial, or a great time of testing then great focus and faith is needed. This private devotional aids in this endeavor.

During these upheaval times in our lives we must focus on trusting in God. We must focus on transitioning into a new creature in Christ.

But Satan does not want this so he uses every influence he has to discourage and derail. You can resist the devil and in time he will flee from you and leave you alone for another day.

Resisting the presence, work and influence of Satan is accomplished by reading God's word, prayer, and meditation upon God's word found in scripture. And it almost always takes 40 days of focus.

This book will help you achieve this focus in all these things during those 40 days.

This private devotion worship book includes scripture focusing on the tremendous wisdom, faith, and instruction found in the Psalms; a brief devotional word; an original praise & worship through spoken word rhyme; and daily biblical promises of focus. A special rhyme prayer is even included daily for you in times when you're not sure what to pray (without sounding repetitive)!

40 day focus on God is vital! But why 40 days?

Just for starters consider these biblically unusual coincidences:

1. Noah saw torrential and devastating rain fall for 40 days. It was a huge time of trial.
2. The Israelites wandered for 40 years in the wilderness as a time of testing.
3. Jesus was tempted in the wilderness 40 days.

Is the number 40 just a coincidence?

Meaning of Number 40

The word "forty" appears 158 times in the King James translation. The number 40 generally symbolizes a period of testing, trial or probation.

It can also mean or symbolize a generation of man. Moses' life, as an example of trial and testing, can be divided up into three blocks of 40 years.

The first 40 years of Moses' life entails him from growing up in Pharaoh's household and living in Egypt until he slays a man and has to flee to Midian. The second part of his life is spent as a shepherd in the wilderness until God calls him at 80 to save his people. During the last third of his life he leads the Israelites out of Egypt and wanders the wilderness until he dies at age 120.

Moses was also on Mount Sinai, on two separate occasions, for 40 days and nights (Exodus 24:18, 34:1 - 28) in order to receive God's laws. He also sent spies, for forty days, to investigate the land God promised the Israelites as an inheritance (Numbers 13:25, 14:34).

Appearances of the Number 40

Because of their sins after leaving Egypt, God swore that the generation of Israelites who left Egyptian bondage would not enter their inheritance in Canaan (Deuteronomy 1). The children of Israel were punished by wandering the wilderness for 40 years before a new generation was allowed to possess the Promised Land.

From the time they entered the Promised Land, to the time of King Saul, Israel was sporadically governed by a number of individuals known as Judges. Though they did not rule like a king, they nevertheless had a tremendous influence on the people, as they represented God and were inspired to execute his will. Judges who served 40 years include Othniel, Deborah and Barak, Eli and Gideon.

The first three human kings over the children of Israel, Saul, David and Solomon, each ruled for forty years (1050 to 930 B.C.).

Abraham tried bargaining with God to not destroy Sodom and Gomorrah if forty righteous people were found within in (Genesis 18:29). Both Isaac and Esau were forty years old when they were first married (Genesis 25:20, 26:34).

Period of Trial or Testing

Elijah went 40 days without food or water at Mount Horeb. Jesus was tempted by the devil many times during the 40 complete days he fasted at the start of his ministry.

After Jesus' resurrection from the dead he appeared to several groups of people over a period of 40 days.

God flooded the earth by having it rain for forty days and nights (Genesis 7:12). After the patriarch Jacob (Israel) died in Egypt, the Egyptians spent forty days embalming his body (Genesis 50:3).

Number 40 and Prophecy

The prophet Jonah powerfully warned ancient Nineveh, for forty days, that its destruction would come because of its many sins (Jonah 3:4).

The prophet Ezekiel was commanded by God to first lay on his left side for 390 days for the Kingdom of Israel. He was then told to lay on his right side for 40 days for the Kingdom of Judah (Ezekiel 4:1 - 6). This act represented, in years, the length each kingdom would suffer correction for their disobedience to God.

The Bible was written by 40 different people. There were 32 writers of the Old Testament and only 8 (Matthew, Mark, Luke, John, James, Peter, Jude, Paul) of the New. I'm sure I'm missing even more "40" sequences but you get the point - the number 40 is key when we talk about revival, testing, and growth.

Clearly, the number 40 is key when it comes to full cycles. Make no mistake about it, when you give your life to Jesus or recommit, you will be tried for 40 days. And sometimes - some people have multiple cycles of 40 day trials because they are continuing to grow and be sanctified by God. But who they turn out to be after that journey ends is far from the person they were when they started that journey.

The Three Temptations of Jesus

The three temptations of Jesus in the wilderness (Matthew 4:1–11; Luke 4:1–13) reveal a layered spiritual battle far deeper than simple physical challenges. Each temptation attacked a core area of Jesus' divine mission, identity, and relationship with the Father.

1. The Temptation to Turn Stones into Bread – Attack on Identity, Trust, and Physical Need

Scripture: "If You are the Son of God, command that these stones become bread." (Matthew 4:3)

Surface level: Hunger and physical need after 40 days of fasting.
Deeper attack: Satan's first assault targeted Jesus' identity and trust in God's provision. The phrase "If You are the Son of God" was a direct challenge to what the Father had just declared at Jesus' baptism — "This is My beloved Son." The enemy was essentially saying, "Prove it. Take matters into your own hands. Don't wait on God."

By tempting Jesus to turn stones to bread, Satan attacked:
• **His physical appetite** — to meet legitimate needs in illegitimate ways.
• **His trust** — urging independence from God's timing.
• **His identity** — questioning the Father's affirmation of who He was.

Jesus resisted by quoting Scripture (Deut. 8:3): *"Man shall not live by bread alone, but by every word that proceeds from the mouth of God."* His reply affirmed that true life is sustained not by provision but by obedient dependence on God.

2. The Temptation to Jump from the Temple – Attack on Faith, Protection, and Presumption

Scripture: "If You are the Son of God, throw Yourself down. For it is written: 'He shall give His angels charge over You.'" (Matthew 4:6)

Surface level: Testing God's promise of protection.
Deeper attack: Satan's second strategy twisted Scripture to push Jesus toward presumption disguised as faith. The temptation was to perform a dramatic miracle to prove divine favor and gain public recognition.

This was an attack on:
• **His faith in God's plan** — tempting Him to force the Father's hand instead of walking by obedience.
• **His humility** — urging Him to display power for personal glory.
• **His reliance on Scripture's full counsel** — Satan quoted Psalm 91 but omitted "in all Your ways," meaning in the path of obedience.

Jesus countered with Deut. 6:16: *"You shall not put the Lord your God to the test."* True faith never manipulates God; it trusts Him even when unseen.

3. The Temptation to Worship Satan for Worldly Power – Attack on Allegiance, Mission, and Glory

Scripture: "All these things I will give You if You will fall down and worship me." (Matthew 4:9)

Surface level: A shortcut to rule the kingdoms of the world.
Deeper attack: The final temptation targeted Jesus' allegiance and mission. Satan offered Him what was rightfully His — the kingdoms of the world — but without the cross, without suffering, without redemption. It was a temptation to gain the crown without Calvary, to embrace glory without obedience.

This was an attack on:
• **His purpose** — tempting Him to abandon the Father's redemptive plan.
• **His allegiance** — calling Him to bow before the usurper rather than the Creator.
• **His worship** — shifting focus from God's glory to worldly gain.

Jesus answered with Deut. 6:13: *"You shall worship the Lord your God, and Him only shall you serve."* His unwavering loyalty to the Father secured the victory Adam lost.

5

Three Waves of Attacks and Temptations On You

Just as Satan tempted Jesus in three escalating waves (appealing first to the flesh, then to pride, then to power), he continues to use the same three-fold pattern on God's people, both individually and globally, especially in the last days. Here's how those three waves of temptation unfold for the followers of Christ:

Wave 1: The Temptation of Bread — The Attack on Dependence and Desire

Focus: Physical needs, appetite, comfort, and survival.
Satan's strategy: To make believers doubt God's care when life gets hard — to push them toward compromise for the sake of convenience or provision.
Modern expression:
• Choosing comfort over conviction ("God understands, I have bills to pay").
• Trading the Sabbath or principles for income, position, or pleasure.
• Allowing anxiety about the economy, inflation, or food shortages to eclipse faith.
Spiritual core: This wave targets the lust of the flesh (1 John 2:16). It whispers, "If God really loved you, why are you struggling? Fix it your own way."
Biblical counter: "Man shall not live by bread alone…" — a reminder that faith depends on God's Word, not worldly security.
End-time application: In times of crisis — famine, financial collapse, or restriction on buying and selling — Satan will pressure believers to choose survival over obedience (Revelation 13:16-17). Those who trust the Lord as Provider will endure.

Wave 2: The Temptation of the Pinnacle — The Attack on Faith and Fame

Focus: Pride, validation, and religious showmanship.
Satan's strategy: To twist spiritual truth into performance — to make believers prove their worth, manipulate God's promises, or seek attention

rather than humility.

Modern expression:
• Building ministries on image instead of intimacy with God.
• Treating faith as a guarantee of personal success.
• Demanding signs, miracles, or emotions before believing.

Spiritual core: This wave targets the pride of life. It whispers, "If you're really blessed, prove it. Show the world what faith looks like."

Biblical counter: "You shall not put the Lord your God to the test." True faith rests quietly in obedience without forcing God's hand.

End-time application: As deception grows, false prophets will showcase counterfeit power and miracle-based religion (Matthew 24:24). Many will fall because they sought spectacle instead of substance.

Wave 3: The Temptation of the Kingdoms — The Attack on Allegiance and Worship

Focus: Power, influence, and the desire to rule or belong to the winning side.

Satan's strategy: To offer earthly gain and security in exchange for loyalty — whether political, economic, or religious.

Modern expression:
• Bowing to cultural pressure for acceptance.
• Blending truth with error to maintain influence.
• Following the crowd instead of standing alone for Christ.

Spiritual core: This wave targets the lust of the eyes — the craving for what the world promises. It whispers, "You can have it all — just bend a little."

Biblical counter: "You shall worship the Lord your God, and Him only shall you serve." Only allegiance to Christ brings eternal victory.

End-time application: Revelation 13 shows this final temptation fully manifested — a global system demanding worship and loyalty. Those who refuse to compromise will be sealed by God, while others accept the mark of the beast for temporary security.

Conclusion

Satan's three waves always follow this arc:
•   Feed yourself = self-sufficiency
•   Prove yourself = self-importance
•   Exalt yourself = self-worship

But Jesus shows the way of victory: dependence, humility, and worship.

Christ served as our example that just as He was tempted, we too will be tried and tempted by the enemy. But just as He was able to withstand fully as a man, we too can withstand - but not alone. We are given divine help and aid - assisted by angels, encouraged by the Holy Spirit, and fully covered by the power and strength of Jesus Himself.

"Every follower of Christ must face the wilderness of testing—tempted in appetite, pride, and power just as Jesus was. But those who, like Him, stand firm and declare, 'It is written,' will see Satan flee in defeat.
And when the dust of battle settles, angels will always draw near to strengthen those who would rather stand with God and be tried,
than fall with the world and be admired."
- Pastor Ed Anderson

When the Worse Occurs

What a joy it is to have the hope that God brings to us because of His Son Jesus. All the promises found in the Bible are ours to claim!

But the fact remains that Satan will bring on trials, tests, and temptations to ALL Christians until they lay to rest in the Lord. It's what Satan is bent on doing. Look at what God says in 1 Peter:

"Be sober [well balanced and self-disciplined], be alert and cautious at all times. That enemy of yours, the devil, prowls around like a roaring lion [fiercely hungry], seeking someone to devour." 1 Peter 5:8 AMP

So all believers must always be watchful and stand ready when the trials and temptations like arrows begin to fly at you!

However, there is one particular time when a person is most vulnerable. It is the days and weeks that follow after a person's baptism.

The Most Vulnerable Time

The time of baptism or rebaptism is a difficult period for many people. In the case of Jesus, His most severe temptations came immediately after His baptism. This trial is often repeated in the experience of people who just gave their life to Jesus through baptism. It is the most vulnerable time.

During this transition time there are many adjustments to be made. For example, frequently the new convert has had close and loving ties with a group of people - some believers and some non-believers. But the journey into deeper spiritual growth often leads to a separation from these dear ones with whom he/she has spent considerable time with and leaves a vacuum that must be filled. He/she must be made to realize at once that there is a new friendship in Jesus and new associations made even more dear with fellow believers.

The baptism may cause severe home problems if others of the family are unsympathetic to this faith development. Although newly baptized people must lean heavily on the Lord, they also need human support and encouragement.

New Christian converts may have been won from the depths of horrible sin. Perhaps they have had bad habits to overcome, vices that long held them in bondage. Now they have found freedom in Christ. It is wonderful! Unfortunately, however, old addictions may not be entirely gone. The battle against sin is not one in which one major victory disposes of the enemy.

Rather, Satan will be even more near. He will study and capitalize on every human weakness. He will try with all his might and influence to bring doubt and discouragement. He will bring a host of new temptations and trials that the new convert to Jesus will need to face. They will question whether their new Christian experience is genuine; whether the whole thing was not a mistake; whether the standards and expectations of him/her are not higher than they can maintain.

At such times it is exceedingly important to focus and drive deeper into prayer, devotion, study, and fellowship with other believers. Many of the backsliding that occur come during the first few days or weeks after baptism.

Many will argue that those who fall away so rapidly probably were not properly instructed, they were brought in too rapidly, or they were never converted in the first place. This thinking is judgmental, false, and disregards the power of the Holy Spirit to bring conversion, this type of thinking places responsibility on action modification and forces one to ask "What more could I do?" Remember, there is nothing a person can do. It's not how much a person does nor how much a person knows that attains salvation, but rather WHO they know that saves. Building a real and honest personal relationship with Jesus is key. And Satan hates it when a person does this! So he attacks. Satan's success rate is higher at this time because he is attacking infant Christians.

There is something that mature Christians can do to help new Christians. Rather than going down the easy path to criticize, not even knowing the vexing circumstances, how much better to make a personal call and seek an opportunity to offer a prayer and encouraging words.

Even mature Christians backslide! It leaves the question, what must newly baptized Christian's do to stay focused on Christ? For the mature Christian, how do they reclaim their spiritual life?

Why Satan Attacks Different Followers of Jesus

Every follower of Christ will face spiritual attack — but the form it takes often depends on where you are in your journey. Satan's schemes are not random; they are strategic, aimed at undermining faith, stealing joy, and silencing the witness of those who walk with God.

The Newly Baptized — Attack on Foundations

When someone emerges from the waters of baptism, heaven rejoices — and hell trembles. Satan attacks quickly because he knows a seed uprooted early never bears fruit. Like Jesus after His baptism, the new believer often faces an immediate wilderness: old temptations resurface, relationships are tested, and faith feels fragile.

He strikes when confidence is new, whispering: "Maybe you weren't ready. Maybe nothing really changed."
But God says, "He who began a good work in you will carry it on to completion." (Philippians 1:6)

The Baptized — Attack on Routine and Resolve

For those who have walked with Jesus for some time, the enemy shifts from shock to subtlety. He no longer tries to overthrow the believer overnight; instead, he lulls them into spiritual sleep. The baptized member may still attend church but lose passion, still serve but without fire.

His aim? To make you busy but barren — doing religious things without renewal, until devotion becomes mere duty.
That's why Paul warned, "Wake up, sleeper… and Christ will shine on you." (Ephesians 5:14)

The Recommitting Follower — Attack on Momentum and Memory

When someone rededicates their life, they become a walking testimony of grace. Satan hates that. He attacks by reviving old guilt and planting new doubt, trying to convince them that their comeback won't last.

He whispers: "You've failed before — you'll fail again."
But Scripture answers: "Though a righteous man falls seven times, he rises again." (Proverbs 24:16)

The recommitted believer must remember: forgiveness erases not just sin but Satan's right to define your story.

The Pastor or Leader — Attack on Influence and Integrity

Leaders stand on the front line of spiritual warfare. When a shepherd is struck, the sheep scatter. That's why pastors face unusual pressure — moral, emotional, and spiritual.

Fatigue, isolation, criticism, and temptation often come not because they are failing but because they are impacting eternity. Satan knows if he can break the leader's integrity, he can wound hundreds of souls at once.
But God reminds every leader: "My grace is sufficient for you, for My strength is made perfect in weakness." (2 Corinthians 12:9)

The Faithful Follower of Jesus — Attack on Perseverance and Purpose

Those who've stood the test of time often face weariness more than wickedness. The devil knows he can't derail their faith easily, so he tries to drain it. Prolonged trials, unanswered prayers, and constant pressure can make even seasoned believers wonder, "Lord, how long?"

But perseverance is the proof of faith. Jesus promised, "He who endures to the end shall be saved." (Matthew 24:13)

A Personal Testimony: When the Battle Hit My Mind

When I was in seminary in the early 1990s, I experienced firsthand how Satan attacks even in moments of devotion. I began having terrible headaches—so severe I could barely think, pray, or focus on my studies. The pain felt like fire in my skull, and there were moments I thought I would lose my mind.

Doctors sent me to Loma Linda University Medical Center, where scans revealed a small brain tumor on the right side of my head above my ear. I'll never forget the fear that gripped me — not just the thought of dying, but of losing the ability to serve God.

But the church prayed. My father prayed. I prayed through tears. Professors, classmates, doctors, and nurses all joined in intercession. When the medical team conducted another MRI, the tumor was gone — completely vanished. The doctors were stunned.

That moment reminded me that Satan often attacks where God is about to work next. He tries to strike the mind that will one day preach, the body that will one day serve, and the soul that will one day testify. Yet every attack can become an altar — a place where God shows His power and turns fear into faith.

Summary Table

Follower Type	Why Satan Attacks	Main Strategy	God's Counter-measure
Newly Baptized	To uproot faith before roots form	Discouragement, temptation	Discipleship and community
Baptized	To turn zeal into routine	Complacency and distraction	Renewal through Word and Spirit
Recommitting	To crush momentum	Guilt and fatigue	Grace and spiritual mentorship
Pastor/Leader	To destroy influence	Pride, exhaustion, moral traps	Prayer covering and accountability
Faithful Follower	To exhaust endurance	Trials, weariness, persecution	Hope in the promise of eternal reward

Why Satan Attacks the Committed

Satan does not waste his weapons on those who pose no threat. His fiercest battles are reserved for those who have decided that half-hearted faith is no longer enough. When a believer goes "all in" for Jesus—fully surrendered, fully available, fully obedient—the enemy sees not just a person, but a divine weapon in God's hands. These are the ones who shake kingdoms, break generational chains, and awaken sleeping churches.

Every follower of Christ carries an assignment—an anointing, a gift, a purpose that heaven designed before birth. The enemy studies these gifts, knowing that a single Spirit-filled life can change entire families, cities, and nations. So he attacks the called, the chosen, the newly baptized, the rebaptized, the recommitted, and the rising leaders—hoping to discourage them before they discover the authority that is already theirs in Christ.

But those who cling to the Word and declare, "It is written," cannot be defeated. They may bend in the storm, but they will not break. For every wilderness trial there are ministering angels waiting on the other side—ready to lift, heal, and strengthen those who refuse to bow. The same Spirit that led Jesus into the wilderness will lead His faithful out—with greater power, deeper faith, and unstoppable purpose.

Satan fears the believer who has learned that pain can't silence praise, that testing can't steal truth, and that obedience—no matter the cost—always ends in victory. Those who stand firm become living testimonies that the cross still conquers, the Word still wins, and Christ still reigns.

Satan's attacks are not signs of abandonment — they are proof of assignment. He only fights those who pose a threat to his kingdom. But the same God who healed in a hospital room, who silenced the tempter in the wilderness, still says today:

"Resist the devil, and he will flee from you." (James 4:7) "And the God of peace will soon crush Satan under your feet." (Romans 16:20)

The Seven Step Spiritual Growth Plan

When the Trials, Testing, and Temptations Come

Every follower of Christ will face seasons of trial, testing, and temptation. These are not signs of abandonment but invitations to grow closer to Jesus. When those dark clouds gather and the storm seems unrelenting, remember this plan—rooted in kindness, love, and faithfulness.

Remember these are not "to do's' to earn salvation or magica encantations to rid yourself of demons, but rather a seven step process to continue focusing on Jesus and rebuking Satan. Eventually, the enemy will know that you are now safe within the walls of God's fortress and it's basically "hands off".

Step 1 - Find a Friend in Jesus

Above all else, turn to Christ. He is not a distant observer but a compassionate friend who understands every sorrow, struggle, and temptation. When your heart is heavy, whisper His name. Speak to Him as you would to a close companion. In His presence, you will find the comfort and strength the world cannot give.

"There is a friend that sticketh closer than a brother." — Proverbs 18:24

Step 2 - Spend Time in Private Prayer and Devotion

Your private moments with God are the anchor of your spiritual life. Set aside quiet time each day to pray, to listen, and to pour out your heart before Him. Prayer is not only asking—it is connecting, aligning, and surrendering. Through personal devotion, you will hear His gentle voice guiding you through the storm.

Step 3 - Open Your Home and Heart

When life feels overwhelming, resist the urge to withdraw completely. Hospitality has healing power. Invite others for a meal, a conversation, or a moment of fellowship. The act of serving others—especially when your own heart is burdened—refreshes your soul and reminds you that love still triumphs over hardship.

Step 4 - Stay Faithful in Worship

The church is more than a building—it's the body of Christ, a refuge for weary hearts. Attend worship services even when you don't feel like it. Sit among God's people, sing, pray, and listen. Look for the stranger who sits alone and make them feel welcome. Don't wait for someone to come to you—be the one who reaches out. Healing often comes through the fellowship of believers.

"Not forsaking the assembling of ourselves together…" — Hebrews 10:25

Step 5 - Serve in Ministry

There is something deeply renewing about serving others. Volunteer in a ministry that aligns with your gifts—whether it's helping children, visiting the sick, or welcoming guests. Service redirects your focus from self to others, turning pain into purpose and sorrow into strength.

Step 6 - Feed on God's Word

When you're weary, your soul needs nourishment. Read the Bible daily, not as a routine, but as a conversation with God. Continue your Bible studies even when distractions come. Each verse is a light for your path and a shield for your heart. The Scriptures remind you of God's promises when fear and doubt whisper lies.

Step 7 - Meditate on the Psalms

The Psalms are God's medicine for the troubled spirit. David's cries, praises, and reflections mirror every human emotion—from despair to triumph. As you meditate on these sacred songs, you will discover that you are not alone in your struggles. Through the Psalms, faith is rekindled, tears are sanctified, and hope is restored.

"The Lord is my rock, and my fortress, and my deliverer." — Psalm 18:2

Remember: Trials are temporary, but character is eternal. Testing reveals what faith can endure. Temptation, when resisted through Christ's strength, becomes a testimony of victory.

So, when the fires come—follow this plan. Let love lead you, prayer ground you, and service renew you. And through it all, hold fast to the One who holds you.

Seven Step Prayer

By Edward O. Anderson, Jr.

Dear Father in heaven,
Thank you for your blessings each day;
Please help us to listen and obey.
Guide us in all that we do;
Help us to trust and lean on you.

May we always choose what is right,
With your wisdom as our guiding light.
Fill our hearts with love and joy,
And keep us safe, each girl and boy.

Help us to be kind and wise,
And treat others with love in our eyes.
In everything we do or say,
Help us bring glory to your name we pray.

For you are our Heavenly King,
And to you, all praises we sing. Amen.

The Healing Voice of Poetry

Finding Strength in Trials, Temptations, and Transitions

Purpose

Poetry has always been the language of the soul—the place where pain and praise meet. When trials test your faith, when temptations whisper to your weakness, and when transitions stretch your courage, poetry becomes a refuge for the spirit. It gives shape to emotions that are too deep for plain speech.

For believers, poetry is more than literature—it's a form of worship. Every verse written in faith becomes a psalm rising from the heart. Poetry slows us down, opens us up, and teaches us to hear God's voice even in silence.

Like David in the Bible, we often discover that some of our deepest theology is written through tears, not textbooks. David's psalms were not written from a palace but from caves and battlefields, in loneliness and repentance, joy and worship. His poetry helped him survive his own trials and reminded him of who God was, even when life fell apart.

"Why art thou cast down, O my soul? and why art thou disquieted within me? Hope thou in God..."— Psalm 42:5

Why Poetry Helps

Poetry gives pain a voice.
When you cannot explain what hurts, poetry gives you a way to speak your truth before God. It's honest, emotional, and freeing.

Poetry slows the soul.
In a world that moves too fast, poetry teaches you to breathe. It invites you to linger with your thoughts and listen for God in the stillness.

Poetry turns theology into intimacy.
Doctrine tells you what God is like. Poetry helps you feel His presence. It transforms your belief into relationship.

Poetry renews perspective.
Every hardship looks smaller when seen through the lens of faith. Poetry helps you rise above the moment and see eternity again.

My Journey with Poetry

A Teenager in Torrance
When I was a high school teen growing up in Torrance, California, I had constant conflict with my father. Our relationship was tense, filled with misunderstandings and unspoken expectations. I didn't know how to express what I felt without causing more friction, so I turned inward.

That's when I discovered songwriting and poetry. Late at night, when the house grew quiet, I'd pull out a notebook and pour out my thoughts in rhyme and rhythm. Those poems became my prayers—sometimes raw, sometimes hopeful—but always real. They helped me process my pain, find my identity, and learn that even in conflict, God was teaching me how to listen, feel, and forgive. What you give in these pages are a collection of over 40 years of poetry written by me over these years.

Poetry became my secret place with God long before I ever learned to preach.

A Seminary Student in Struggle
Years later, in seminary, I found myself wrestling with two of the most intimidating subjects imaginable—Greek and Hebrew. They were beautiful languages, but for me, they felt like climbing Mount Everest every day. I remember long nights staring at verb charts, feeling utterly defeated.

Then one evening, I prayed, "Lord, if David could write psalms in his trials, maybe I can write mine in mine." So I began composing short psalms of my own—simple lines of poetry that turned frustration into faith.

Each poem became a conversation with God. Somehow, through the rhythm of writing and the discipline of devotion, the chaos cleared. My thoughts aligned, my focus sharpened, and my heart calmed. The result? Not only did I pass, but by God's grace, I graduated top of my class with a perfect 4.0 GPA.

Poetry didn't just help me pass—it helped me pray my way through the im-

possible. Again, on these pages are poems written during these trying times.
When Disaster Hit
Then came one of the darkest valleys of my life. In the late 1990s, my family faced a devastating crisis—one that left me broken, disoriented, and questioning everything. I had three choices: end it, suffer from it, or grow from it.

By God's grace, I chose to grow. But growth didn't come easily—it came through tears, songs, and poems. I began to write again, this time from the depths of grief. The words that poured out were sometimes messy, sometimes mournful—but they were also healing.

Poetry and music became the twin lights that led me out of despair. In writing, I rediscovered purpose. In rhythm, I found restoration. And in those sacred creative moments, I felt God whisper again: "I'm not finished with you yet."

What had been disaster became a divine reset. My brokenness became the birthplace of ministry. In these pages you will poems written by me during these long days and nights.

How to Use the Poetry in This Devotional

Each devotion in this book includes a short reflection and an original poem written by me—born out of life's very real struggles. These poems are not just verses; they are testimonies wrapped in rhythm, faith, and prayer.

Here's how to make the most of them:
- **Read Slowly.** Don't rush. Let the poem speak to your soul.
- **Pray Honestly.** Turn the lines into your own conversation with God.
- **Reflect Deeply.** Write down your thoughts, emotions, or even your own poem in response.
- **Share Freely.** If a verse touches you, share it with someone who needs hope.

Each page is a spiritual mirror   a place for your heart to meet God's pres ence through poetry.

When the Night Is Long
By Edward O. Anderson, Jr.

When shadows press and faith feels thin,
And doubts crowd loud where peace has been,
I lift my gaze where mercy stays—
The God who writes through all my days.

The stars still shine through clouds of fear,
Their whispered light says, "I am near."
Though tears may fall, they will not stay,
For morning waits with songs of day.

So here I'll rest where grace abides,
Beneath love's wings, my soul will hide.
And though the night seems cold and long,
My heart will heal in Heaven's song.

Final Reflection

Poetry is the soul's candle in the darkness. It teaches us that faith doesn't deny pain—it transforms it. When the night feels endless, remember: even your tears can become lyrics of hope in God's songbook of grace.

Poetry is how the heart learns to breathe when the world feels suffocating. It is prayer with rhythm, worship with tears, and truth wrapped in tenderness.

Whether you're facing conflict, study, or catastrophe—like David—you can find healing in holy words. And as you do, remember:

You are not just reading poetry.
You are becoming one—
God's living, breathing poem of grace.

A Visual Journey: Reading Between the Lines

Designed and Illustrated by Pastor Ed Anderson
Every image you encounter in this book was prayerfully designed to do more than decorate the page — it's meant to speak to your spirit. Each graphic, illustration, and symbol was created by me, blending visual story-telling with spiritual depth.

These are not stock images or filler art — they are windows into another world. Every stroke, color, and texture carries meaning. Each design was inspired by moments of prayer, devotion, and creativity in the creation of this book — merging faith and imagination to awaken wonder within the reader.

When you turn the pages, pause. Look closer.

You might notice something you didn't see before — a hidden symbol, a subtle light source, a small engraving of a cross, a path, or a whisper of Scripture woven into the background. They invite you to search for spiritual truths the way a child hunts for treasure — joyfully, attentively, and with open eyes.

How to Experience the Art

Transport Your Mind to a Different Time and Place.
Let your imagination travel. Each image carries echoes of biblical history, future hope, and timeless truth. Ask: What story might this picture be telling me?

Read the Image as You Read Scripture.
Don't rush past it. Observe the colors, the light, the shadow, the symbolism. Transport yourself into the picture. Like the parables of Jesus, what's visible often hides a deeper truth.

Reflect and Pray.
Art has a way of softening the heart and focusing the mind. Let each design stir reflection. Sometimes what the eye sees can awaken what the soul has forgotten.

24

The Purpose of Visual Devotion

Words reach the mind, but art reaches the heart. That's why Jesus painted with parables — using imagery to invite people into revelation. Likewise, every design in this book aims to do the same: to remind you that faith is not only heard but also seen.

These pages are meant to be more than read — they are meant to be experienced.

So take your time. Linger. Let the art breathe.

Each illustration tells a story, and each story leads you closer to the One who is the Master Artist Himself.

"For we are His workmanship,
created in Christ Jesus unto good works…"
— Ephesians 2:10

Why These Devotions Are Arranged in This Sequence

Every storm of life follows a rhythm:

fear first rises, then
weakness follows, then
anxiety grows, then
darkness deepens, and then,

slowly, **faith returns**,
strength rebuilds, and
light breaks through.

The Top 40 "While in the Storm" Bible Texts of Hope are not simply forty random verses of comfort. They are intentionally ordered as a spiritual journey from panic to peace, from trembling to triumph.

When you begin this devotional sequence, you'll notice that the early readings meet you in the place of crisis—when fear surrounds you. These passages anchor your heart when the winds first begin to howl.

As you move forward, the next group of texts—when you feel weak or overwhelmed—invites you to lean not on your own strength but on the power of God's grace. Then, when anxiety or worry rises, Scripture gently trains your mind to rest, reminding you that peace comes not from control but from surrender.

But the journey doesn't stop there.

In the middle of the storm, when darkness seems endless, the Word becomes light itself—reminding you that morning always follows midnight. From that light, your faith begins to rise again.

You enter the season of believing without seeing—holding fast when all you have left is hope. And when loneliness sets in, when you feel alone, the verses whisper that you are never truly by yourself; the Presence walks beside you even when no one else can.

Finally, the last two sections—remembering God's power and waiting for breakthrough—are written for those moments when you've endured the storm and are waiting for the clouds to clear.

These verses shift the focus from survival to surrender, from endurance to expectation. They remind you that storms are not the end of your story—they are the setting for God's greatest miracles.

Together, these categories form more than a devotional outline—they form a map of the soul's journey through the storm.

From fear to faith, from chaos to calm, from despair to divine peace, each text moves you one step closer to the voice that still says:

"Peace, be still."

When Fear Surrounds You

When the storm's waves rise higher than your courage, remember — the One who walks on water is not far away. Even when you tremble, His voice still calms the sea and your soul.

Day 01 - Through the Waters, Not Overwhelmed

"When you pass through the waters, I will be with you; and through the rivers, they shall not overflow you."
— Isaiah 43:2

Storms have a way of revealing what's real. They strip away illusions of control and force us to confront what we truly trust in.

God never promised that His children would avoid deep waters—but He did promise His presence in them. *"When* you pass through the waters," He says—not *"if"*.

The word *through* is crucial. It means the storm isn't final; it's a passage. The waters may rise, the current may pull, but they will not take you under, because the One who walks on water walks beside you.

Consider the story of Winston Churchill during the darkest days of World War II. London was burning from bombings, morale was collapsing, and hope seemed lost. Yet Churchill stood before the British people and declared, *"We shall never surrender."*

Those weren't just words of defiance—they were words of faith in endurance. He knew that survival wasn't the absence of struggle; it was the courage to stand firm in it. In the same way, God calls us to a steady, storm-defying faith—to trust that His presence is stronger than any flood.

When you feel the waters rising around your soul, don't panic. Lift your eyes to the One who promises, *"I will be with you."* The same God who parted the Red Sea, who calmed the storm on Galilee, still speaks peace over your chaos.

You may be soaked by sorrow and shaken by fear, but you will not drown in despair. The storm you're in today will one day be the testimony you tell tomorrow—proof that grace carried you safely through.

Through the Waters

By Edward O. Anderson, Jr.
(Inspired by Isaiah 43:2)

When waves arise and tempests roar,
And fear beats hard against my door,
O Lord of peace, my heart renew—
You walk the storm; You see me through.

The rivers rise, the currents strain,
But You are near in wind and rain.
Your hand upholds when I am weak,
Your whisper calms the words I speak.

Though oceans swell and shadows stay,
Your light still marks my narrow way.
No flood shall drown what faith has grown,
For I am Yours, and Yours alone.

So lead me, Lord, through storm and sea,
Your promise stands, my guarantee.
Through every tide my heart shall sing—
You are my refuge, my everything.

Daily Reflection:
Through the Waters

Promise Text: "When you pass through the waters, I will be with you; and through the rivers, they shall not overflow you." — Isaiah 43:2

1. What "waters" am I passing through right now—what trial, temptation, or battle feels like it's threatening to pull me under? (Be specific—name it. Identifying your storm helps you invite God into it.)

2. Where can I recognize God's presence in this situation, even if I don't feel Him? (What signs, people, Scriptures, or small mercies remind me that He's walking beside me through it?)

3. What might God be teaching or strengthening in me as I walk through—not around—this storm? (How could this trial deepen my faith, refine my trust, or redirect my steps toward Him?)

Write your answers above or in a separate journal and date it with today's date. Now give and leave it with the Lord.

Day 02 - The Refuge That Never Fails

"God is our refuge and strength, a very present help in trouble.
Therefore will not we fear…"
— Psalm 46:1–2

When everything around you shakes, the safest place isn't an escape—it's the presence of God. The psalmist doesn't say God "gives" refuge; he says God *is* our refuge.

He's not a distant fortress on a faraway hill; He's a shelter that surrounds your soul right where you stand. The storms of life may rage, the mountains may tremble, and the ground may shift, but God remains unmoved.

He is not only a refuge for your circumstances but also strength for your heart. When fear shouts loudest, faith whispers, *"Therefore will not we fear."*

History offers many who clung to that truth, but few like Corrie ten Boom, a Dutch Christian who hid Jews during the Holocaust. She and her family were arrested and sent to Ravensbrück concentration camp.

Surrounded by cruelty and death, Corrie discovered that even in a place built to destroy faith, God's presence could still be found. She later wrote, *"There is no pit so deep that God's love is not deeper still."* Her unbreakable spirit was not the absence of fear, but the triumph of faith in a refuge stronger than steel or stone.

Whatever storm you face—grief, betrayal, sickness, or uncertainty—God's promise stands: He is very present.

Not someday, not only when you're strong, but now. When the night is longest, His nearness becomes your anchor. So breathe deep, lift your eyes, and rest in this truth: the winds may howl, but the Refuge remains. The One who helped yesterday will not fail you today.

My Refuge and Strength

By Edward O. Anderson, Jr.
(Inspired by Psalm 46:1–2)

When shadows fall and fears appear,
Lord, You are close—my refuge near.
Though mountains quake and oceans roar,
Your steadfast love will hold once more.

When life unravels, hearts grow weak,
Your whisper stills the storm I seek.
You are my fortress, sure and wide,
My shelter strong, where I can hide.

The earth may shake, the sky may tear,
But I will rest—I will not fear.
For You, O Lord, are ever near,
My strength, my song, my refuge here.

When all around me seems undone,
I'll trust the God who never runs.
Through every trial, deep or long,
You are my refuge—my strength, my song.

Daily Reflection:
My Refuge and Strength

Promise Text: "God is our refuge and strength, a very present help in trouble. Therefore will not we fear..." — Psalm 46:1–2

1. Where in my life right now do I feel most under pressure, afraid, or out of control—and how might God be inviting me to take refuge in Him instead of my own strength? (Identify the situation or emotion that most challenges your peace.)

2. How have I experienced God's presence in past troubles, and what can that memory teach me about trusting Him in today's storm? (Think of a time when God's help came just when you needed it.)

3. What would change in my heart, my choices, or my words if I truly believed that God is "very present" in my current battle right now? (Reflect on how faith in His nearness could transform your fear into confidence.)

Write your answers above or in a separate journal and date it with today's date. Now give and leave it with the Lord.

Day 03 - When the Master Speaks Peace

"And He arose, and rebuked the wind, and said unto the sea, Peace, be still. And the wind ceased, and there was a great calm."
— Mark 4:39

Every storm has a voice. Sometimes it's the voice of fear whispering, "You're not going to make it." Other times, it's the noise of doubt, guilt, or grief that roars inside your mind.

The disciples heard that storm on the Sea of Galilee and panicked, thinking they were perishing—until Jesus stood up. The same Jesus who slept in the storm rose and spoke to it. He didn't argue with the wind or reason with the waves—He simply said, *"Peace, be still."* Instantly, nature bowed in obedience.

The lesson is timeless: when Jesus speaks, chaos surrenders.

A century ago, Horatio Spafford lived this verse in the most heartbreaking way. After losing his four daughters in a shipwreck across the Atlantic, he boarded another vessel to meet his grieving wife.

When the captain pointed out the spot where the tragedy occurred, Spafford went to his cabin and penned the immortal words, *"When peace like a river attendeth my way, when sorrows like sea billows roll; whatever my lot, Thou hast taught me to say, It is well with my soul."*

The storm outside him was devastating, but the Savior within him spoke peace stronger than death itself.

When life's waves threaten to pull you under, remember: peace isn't found in the absence of storms, but in the presence of Jesus. He doesn't always remove the wind immediately—but He always rules over it.

And when His voice echoes through your soul, every anxious tide must bow to His authority. The same Jesus who calmed the sea still whispers today, *"Peace, be still."*

Peace, Be Still

By Edward so. Anderson, Jr.
(Inspired by Mark 4:39)

When waves arise and fears resound,
When faith feels lost and hope's unbound,
O Lord who calms the raging sea,
Speak once again Your peace to me.

The storm may shout, the winds may roar,
But You command the ocean's floor.
No power of night, no wave of sin,
Can silence peace when You speak in.

My trembling heart, O Savior, still—
Teach me to trust Your perfect will.
When chaos reigns and courage dies,
Let *"Peace, be still"* be my reply.

So when the tempests test my soul,
And thunder shakes beyond control,
I'll rest, assured, beneath Your care—
The storm obeys when You are there.

Daily Reflection:
Peace, Be Still

Promise Text: "And He arose, and rebuked the wind, and said unto the sea, Peace, be still. And the wind ceased, and there was a great calm." — Mark 4:39

1. What "storm" is raging most fiercely in my life right now—anxiety, temptation, loss, or conflict—and how have I been reacting to it? (Am I trying to row harder, or am I inviting Jesus into the boat?)

2. Where might I need to let Jesus speak "Peace, be still" into my heart today? (What thoughts, fears, or emotions need to be quieted by His voice?)

3. If I truly believed that Christ has authority over every wind and wave in my life, how would that change the way I face my current battle? (What would it look like to rest, rather than react, in His presence?)

Write your answers above or in a separate journal and date it with today's date. Now give and leave it with the Lord.

Day 04 - Safe Beneath His Wings

"He shall cover thee with His feathers,
and under His wings shalt thou trust."
— *Psalm 91:4*

There is something tender and powerful about the image of God covering His children with His wings. It's a picture of both protection and intimacy—of a God who draws us close when life grows cold and dangerous.

The psalmist invites us to imagine the Almighty not as a distant king, but as a nurturing parent-bird shielding its young from the storm. The wind may howl, the rain may fall, but under His wings, you are safe.

Fear may pound at the edges of your faith, yet the warmth of His presence remains constant.

During the early days of the Civil Rights Movement, Dr. Martin Luther King Jr. lived this verse daily. After receiving a string of death threats and watching his home bombed, he felt fear pressing in on every side.

One night, exhausted and trembling, he prayed at his kitchen table, confessing to God that he was at the end of his strength. He later recounted hearing an inner voice say, "Stand up for righteousness, stand up for truth, and I will be with you until the end."

In that moment, peace washed over him—a divine covering that no human threat could penetrate. From that night forward, he faced every danger knowing he was sheltered beneath the wings of an Almighty God.

When you feel exposed, remember this promise: God's wings are wide enough for your fears, your failures, and your future. His covering doesn't always remove the storm, but it keeps you steady through it.

Trust in His embrace. Rest in His feathers. And when the thunder rolls, you'll discover the quiet truth that His wings are stronger than the storm itself.

Beneath His Wings

By Edward O. Anderson, Jr.
(Inspired by Psalm 91:4)

When fear takes flight and shadows fall,
Your wings of mercy cover all.
No storm, no night, no darkened sky,
Can hide me from Your watchful eye.

You spread Your grace, a shelter wide,
Where weary hearts in peace abide.
Though arrows fly and tempests sting,
My soul finds rest beneath Your wing.

So teach me, Lord, to trust, not flee,
To dwell where You would cover me.
For safety lives where love still clings—
Forever kept beneath Your wings.

Daily Reflection:
Beneath His Wings

Promise Text: "He shall cover thee with His feathers, and under His wings shalt thou trust." — Psalm 91:4

1. What fears, worries, or situations make me feel most exposed or unprotected right now—and how might God be inviting me to rest under His covering instead of striving on my own? (Think about where you've been trying to fight the storm rather than rest beneath His shelter.)

2. What does it mean for me personally to "trust under His wings"? (Is there a step of faith, surrender, or patience God is asking of me?)

3. Where have I seen God's protective hand in my past—times when I didn't even realize He was shielding me? (Remembering His faithfulness in the past strengthens trust for today.)

Write your answers above or in a separate journal and date it with today's date. Now give and leave it with the Lord.

Day 05 - The Peace That Stays

"Peace I leave with you, My peace I give unto you…
Let not your heart be troubled, neither let it be afraid."
— John 14:27

Jesus spoke these words on the eve of His greatest trial. The disciples' world was about to collapse—betrayal, arrest, and crucifixion lay just hours ahead. Yet in that moment of looming darkness, Jesus didn't promise escape; He promised peace.

Not the fragile kind that depends on circumstances, but a divine calm that remains when the world falls apart. His peace isn't the absence of trouble—it's the presence of Christ within the trouble.

When your heart feels anxious, remember that the peace Jesus gives is not borrowed from this world—it's anchored in eternity.

That same peace sustained Nelson Mandela through 27 years of imprisonment on Robben Island. Deprived of freedom, family, and basic dignity, Mandela refused to let hatred or despair rule his heart.

Instead, he found an inner calm through prayer, reflection, and forgiveness. *"As I walked out the door toward my freedom,"* he later said, *"I knew that if I didn't leave my bitterness and hatred behind, I'd still be in prison."* His peace was not political—it was spiritual. It was the kind of peace only God can give—the peace that guards your heart when everything else is taken away.

When the storms of life threaten to unsettle you, hold fast to Jesus' words: *"My peace I give unto you."* It's a peace that the world cannot understand and the enemy cannot steal.

You may not be able to change your surroundings, but through Christ, you can change your spirit within them.

Breathe in His promise, release your fear, and rest in the truth that the peace He left is still yours to live in today.

The Peace You Give

By Edward O. Anderson, Jr.
(Inspired by John 14:27)

When fear surrounds and faith feels small,
Your voice still whispers over all.
Not as the world gives—swift to flee,
But deep, abiding peace from Thee.

When anxious thoughts my mind confound,
Your stillness speaks—no safer sound.
Lord, calm the waves that roar within,
And make me whole where storms have been.

Let not my heart with worry ache,
For You are peace no power can shake.
In every trial, I'll rest and live—
At ease within the peace You give.

Daily Reflection:
The Peace You Give

Promise Text: "Peace I leave with you, My peace I give unto you… Let not your heart be troubled, neither let it be afraid." — John 14:27

1. What is currently troubling or unsettling my heart, and how have I been trying to manage it on my own instead of resting in Christ's peace? (Identify the source of your inner storm so you can invite Jesus into it.)

2. How is the peace that Jesus gives different from the temporary peace the world offers? (Consider how His peace remains steady even when circumstances do not.)

3. What practical step can I take today to let go of fear and receive Christ's peace more fully? (It might be prayer, worship, a pause for gratitude, or choosing silence over worry.)

Write your answers above or in a separate journal and date it with today's date. Now give and leave it with the Lord.

When You Feel Weak or Overwhelmed

When your strength fades and your hands grow tired, God's strength takes over. His grace doesn't remove your weakness — it redeems it, turning your exhaustion into evidence of His power.

Day 06 - Strength in the Broken Places

"My grace is sufficient for thee: for My strength is made perfect in weakness."
— *2 Corinthians 12:9*

God doesn't always calm the storm—sometimes He steadies His child in the middle of it. When Paul pleaded for his "thorn in the flesh" to be removed, he received an answer that defied expectation: *"My grace is sufficient for thee."*

Grace doesn't always change what's happening around us; it transforms what's happening within us. It's the quiet power that allows us to endure when we'd rather escape, to keep standing when we should have fallen, and to find purpose in our pain.

The very place we feel weakest often becomes the clearest window for God's strength to shine through.

A striking example of this truth is Nick Vujicic, the Australian-born evangelist who came into the world without arms or legs. As a child, he wrestled with deep depression and feelings of hopelessness. But when he encountered Christ's grace, his life was transformed.

Nick learned that while he couldn't change his physical condition, he could let God use it to change hearts. Today, he speaks to millions around the world about hope, courage, and faith. He once said, "If God can use a man without arms and legs to be His hands and feet, then He will certainly use any willing heart." Nick's life is living proof that grace doesn't remove weakness—it redeems it.

When you feel limited, broken, or overwhelmed, remember: God's grace isn't delayed—it's already sufficient. Your weakness isn't a disqualification; it's an invitation for divine strength.

So, let your frailty become your altar and your struggle become your song. Because when you lean into grace, you'll discover that His strength has been waiting to carry you all along.

Sufficient Grace

By Edward O. Anderson, Jr.
(Inspired by 2 Corinthians 12:9)

When I am weak and strength is gone,
Your grace, O Lord, keeps pressing on.
When mountains rise I cannot climb,
Your mercy lifts me every time.

I bring my thorns, my fears, my pain,
You turn them all to holy gain.
For in my lack, Your love abides—
Your strength made perfect where I hide.

So let me rest, though trials stay,
Your grace is new with every day.
I'll boast in weakness, not in might,
For grace has turned my dark to light.

Daily Reflection:
My Grace Is Sufficient

Promise Text: "My grace is sufficient for thee: for My strength is made perfect in weakness." — 2 Corinthians 12:9

1. What "thorn" or area of weakness am I asking God to remove—and could He be using it to reveal His strength in me instead? (Reflect on how difficulty can become a doorway for divine power.)

2. How has God's grace sustained me in times when I felt completely un-qualified, unprepared, or undone? (Remember specific moments when His strength carried you farther than your own could.)

3. What would it look like for me to stop hiding my weakness and start boasting in God's grace through it? (How could my transparency encourage others to trust Him more deeply?)

Write your answers above or in a separate journal and date it with today's date. Now give and leave it with the Lord.

Day 07 - Strength for the Climb

"I can do all things through Christ which strengtheneth me."
— Philippians 4:13

The Apostle Paul wrote these words not from a place of comfort, but from a prison cell. His declaration wasn't about superhuman ability—it was about supernatural endurance. "I can do all things" meant that whether he faced hunger or abundance, chains or freedom, he could endure every circumstance through Christ's power at work within him.

This verse isn't a slogan for success—it's a lifeline for survival. It reminds us that strength isn't the absence of struggle, but the presence of Jesus in it.

True strength is not what you lift with your hands, but what you carry in your heart when you refuse to give up because He hasn't given up on you.

Few people have embodied this truth like Bethany Hamilton, the professional surfer who lost her arm in a shark attack at the age of thirteen. Her dream was nearly destroyed in an instant—but her faith held firm.

Within months, she was back in the ocean, learning to balance on her board and trust the God who gave her new purpose. Bethany later said, "I don't need easy; I just need possible—and through God, all things are possible."

Her story is not about overcoming tragedy by willpower, but about leaning on the sustaining power of Christ. She discovered what Paul meant: strength doesn't come from what you have—it comes from Who holds you.

When the waves of life threaten to pull you under, remember that your strength isn't measured by your ability—it's multiplied by His grace. You don't have to face today's challenges alone.

The same Christ who empowered Paul in prison and Bethany on the waves will empower you in your own storm. His strength isn't distant—it's already within you.

Strength Through Christ

By Edward O. Anderson, Jr.
(Inspired by Philippians 4:13)

When life feels heavy, hope seems small,
Your strength, O Lord, can lift it all.
When doors are closed and dreams grow dim,
I'll find my courage still in Him.

Not by my power, nor by my might,
But through Your grace and endless light.
When faith runs low and fears take hold,
Your promise makes my spirit bold.

I can do all, through Christ, my stay—
Who gives me strength for every day.
So help me rise, though mountains steep,
For in Your strength, my soul shall keep.

Daily Reflection:
Strength Through Christ

Promise Text: "I can do all things through Christ which strengtheneth me."
— Philippians 4:13

1. What challenge or "mountain" in my life right now feels too steep to climb on my own strength? (How might God be inviting me to depend more deeply on Him instead of myself?)

2. When have I experienced Christ's strength carrying me through something I thought I couldn't endure? (Recall a past trial that proves His faithfulness.)

3. What would change in my attitude, prayers, or actions if I truly believed Christ's power is already within me? (Consider how this truth could reshape your confidence and courage today.)

Write your answers above or in a separate journal and date it with today's date. Now give and leave it with the Lord.

Day 08 - Rising Above the Storm

"But they that wait upon the Lord shall renew their strength;
they shall mount up with wings as eagles; they shall run, and not be weary;
and they shall walk, and not faint."
— Isaiah 40:31

Waiting is rarely easy, especially when you're weary, wounded, or wondering if God still remembers your name. Yet Isaiah reminds us that waiting on the Lord is not passive—it's a posture of trust.

To "wait" in Hebrew means to hope with expectancy, to lean forward in faith. Those who do so will find their strength renewed—not borrowed from the world, but breathed in by the Spirit.

God doesn't promise to remove every mountain; He promises to give you wings to rise above it. Like an eagle soaring higher on the same winds that trouble lesser birds, you will find that the storm designed to break you is the very wind that lifts you closer to Him.

A living example of this truth is Elisabeth Elliot, whose husband, missionary Jim Elliot, was killed by the very tribe they came to serve in Ecuador. Crushed by grief, she could have given up—but instead, she waited on God. In time, that same tribe invited her to live among them, and through her quiet faith and forgiveness, many came to know Christ.

She later wrote, *"God never withholds from His child that which His love and wisdom call good."* Elisabeth's waiting wasn't wasted—it was worship. Through her patient endurance, she discovered the kind of strength that only comes from resting in God's timing.

When your energy fades and your heart feels faint, don't give up—look up. The eagle doesn't fight the wind; it uses it.

So too, your storm may be the very force God uses to lift you to higher faith. Wait on Him. Hope in Him. You will rise again—stronger, steadier, and closer to Heaven than before.

Wings of Faith

By Edward O. Anderson, Jr.
(Inspired by Isaiah 40:31)

When all my strength has slipped away,
And darkness steals the light of day,
Lord, teach my heart to trust, not strive,
For in Your hope, my soul's alive.

I'll wait on You through wind and rain,
Till faith takes flight above my pain.
Like eagles soar on wings renewed,
Your strength becomes my altitude.

So lift me, Lord, beyond the storm,
Where peace and purpose both are born.
I'll rise with You, my heart set free—
My strength restored, my eyes on Thee.

Daily Reflection:
Waiting and Rising

Promise Text: "But they that wait upon the Lord shall renew their strength…" — Isaiah 40:31

1. What area of my life feels like an exhausting wait—and how might God be using this delay to strengthen my faith rather than discourage it? (Consider how waiting can deepen trust and maturity.)

2. Am I trying to rush ahead of God's timing instead of resting in His renewal? (Reflect on how impatience may be draining your spiritual energy.)

3. What would it look like for me to "mount up with wings as eagles" this week? (Is there a situation where I need to shift from struggling below the storm to rising above it in faith?)

Write your answers above or in a separate journal and date it with today's date. Now give and leave it with the Lord.

Day 09 - When the Heart Breaks, God Draws Near

*"The Lord is nigh unto them that are of a broken heart;
and saveth such as be of a contrite spirit."*
— Psalm 34:18

A broken heart can make the world feel silent and God seem far away. Yet Scripture tells us the opposite is true—when life shatters, God draws closer. His nearness isn't always loud or dramatic; sometimes it's the quiet strength that helps you take one more breath, one more step, one more prayer.

The Hebrew word for "nigh" in this verse means *intimately near*—God doesn't watch your pain from a distance; He enters it with you. The same hands that shaped galaxies now cradle your grief.

Brokenness doesn't repel God—it attracts Him.

The life of C.S. Lewis reveals this truth beautifully. Known for his intellect and imagination, Lewis faced devastating loss when his dear beloved wife, Joy Davidman, died of cancer. His grief was raw and unfiltered—he even confessed that it felt as if "the door of heaven had been slammed in my face."

Yet as he wrestled with sorrow, he discovered a deeper intimacy with God. In his book *A Grief Observed*, Lewis later wrote, *"You never know how much you really believe anything until its truth or falsehood becomes a matter of life and death."* Through the breaking, his faith was refined, and he came to see that God's presence in pain was more real than ever before.

When your heart aches and tears blur your faith, remember—God is not far; He's closer than your next heartbeat. His comfort doesn't erase the sorrow, but it transforms it into sacred ground where healing begins.

The same God who met David in the caves, Lewis in his grief, and Jesus in Gethsemane will meet you right where you are. You may be broken, but you are not alone.

In your shattered places, Heaven bends low—and the Lord is near.

When My Heart Is Broken

By Edward O. Anderson, Jr.

(Inspired by Psalm 34:18)

When tears fall down and words grow few,
Lord, draw me close—Your love is true.
My heart is crushed, my spirit sore,
Yet still You whisper, *"I am more."*

You gather pain and turn it mild,
You hold the hurt, You heal the child.
No wound too deep, no night too long,
For near to me, You make me strong.

So in the dark, I'll trust Your name,
Your nearness shines through all my pain.
The Lord who mends what sorrow breaks—
Will lift me up when morning wakes.

Daily Reflection:
When the Heart Breaks

Promise Text: "The Lord is nigh unto them that are of a broken heart; and saveth such as be of a contrite spirit." — Psalm 34:18

1. Where do I feel most broken, weary, or unseen right now—and how can I invite God into that place instead of hiding it? (Let honesty become the doorway to healing.)

2. When have I experienced God's nearness in a season of pain or loss? (Remember moments when comfort came quietly, reminding you that you were not alone.)

3. How might my current brokenness become a bridge to help someone else who is hurting? (God often uses the places we've been wounded to bring healing to others.)

Write your answers above or in a separate journal and date it with today's date. Now give and leave it with the Lord.

Day 10 - Steady Feet on Shaky Ground

"The Lord God is my strength, and He will make my feet like hinds' feet,
and He will make me to walk upon mine high places."
— Habakkuk 3:19

When the world beneath you shakes, it's easy to lose your footing. Habakkuk knew this feeling well—his nation was collapsing, his prayers seemed unanswered, and fear filled the air. Yet instead of despairing, he declared, *"The Lord God is my strength."*

The image of "hinds' feet" refers to the sure-footed deer that climbs steep, dangerous cliffs with ease. God may not remove your mountain, but He will give you the balance and endurance to climb it.

Strength doesn't always mean running fast—it means standing steady when everything around you moves. When you depend on the Lord, you find the grace to walk where you once would have fallen.

This truth shines in the life of Helen Keller, who lost her sight and hearing at nineteen months old. For years, she lived in a world of silence and darkness until her teacher, Anne Sullivan, broke through with patience and love.

Helen could have surrendered to despair, but instead, she pressed forward in faith. Through discipline, learning, and courage, she mastered language, graduated from college, and inspired millions around the world. She once wrote, *"Character cannot be developed in ease and quiet. Only through experience of trial and suffering can the soul be strengthened."* Helen learned to climb life's steepest cliffs through God's strength—her hind's feet found footing on heights she never imagined.

When your path feels uncertain, remember: God is shaping your steps for higher ground. The storm beneath you may roar, but His strength within you remains unshaken.

Trust Him to make you sure-footed. What once looked like defeat will become the very place where His strength lifts you upward.

Hinds' Feet and Holy Ground

By Edward O. Anderson, Jr.
(Inspired by Habakkuk 3:19)

When mountains rise and paths grow steep,
And faith feels small, too weak to keep,
Lord, be my strength, my guiding light,
My feet made sure on peaks of height.

Though rocks may shift and storms may call,
Your steady hand will guard my fall.
I'll climb with grace, though winds may blow,
For You, O Lord, have made it so.

Each step I take, each tear I cry,
Will lift me closer to the sky.
For You, my strength, my solid ground,
Make hinds' feet sure where hope is found.

Daily Reflection:
Walking on High Places

Promise Text: "The Lord God is my strength, and He will make my feet like hinds' feet…" — Habakkuk 3:19

1. What "mountain" or challenge am I facing right now that feels too steep to climb—and how might God be strengthening me through it? (Reflect on how endurance is often built through struggle, not ease.)

2. Where have I seen God give me stability or peace in situations that once made me stumble? (Look back at moments of quiet resilience—evidence of His strength within you.)

3. How can I shift from asking God to remove the mountain to asking Him to make my feet sure upon it? (Consider what faith looks like when it chooses perseverance over escape.)

Write your answers above or in a separate journal and date it with today's date. Now give and leave it with the Lord.

When Anxiety or Worry Rises

Anxiety may shout, but peace whispers louder when you listen for God's heart. Surrender what you can't control, and rest in the arms of the One who never sleeps.

Day 11 - Letting Go into His Hands

"Casting all your care upon Him; for He careth for you."
— *1 Peter 5:7*

Worry is a weight the soul was never meant to carry. Yet we clutch it tightly—our anxieties, deadlines, fears, and regrets—hoping somehow to control the uncontrollable.

Peter reminds us that faith is not holding tighter, but letting go. The word casting here means to throw or hurl away, as one would cast a heavy burden off their shoulders. God doesn't ask us to manage our cares; He asks us to give them to Him—because He genuinely cares for us.

His care is not distant sympathy but active involvement. When we surrender our struggles into His hands, we discover that His strength is already beneath them.

A vivid example of this truth is found in George Müller, the 19th-century evangelist who cared for over 10,000 orphans in Bristol, England. Müller never made his needs publicly known—he simply prayed. Time and again, when the cupboards were bare and funds gone, he cast his cares upon God.

One morning, with no food left, he gathered the children for breakfast and prayed, thanking God for the meal He would provide. Moments later, a baker knocked on the door, saying God had prompted him to bring fresh bread, followed by a milkman whose cart had broken down outside, offering milk to everyone. Müller once said, *"The beginning of anxiety is the end of faith, and the beginning of true faith is the end of anxiety."*

When your heart feels heavy and your mind restless, remember—you are not meant to carry it alone. God's care is personal, present, and powerful.

Every care you release becomes a channel for His peace to flow. So, lift your hands, loosen your grip, and cast it all upon Him. The same God who fed orphans, calmed storms, and carried the cross can surely carry you.

Into Your Hands

By Edward O. Anderson, Jr.
(Inspired by 1 Peter 5:7)

The weight I've held so long, so tight,
Has robbed my days and stilled my light.
But now, O Lord, I lay it down—
Each fear, each care, each heavy crown.

You care for me—how deep, how true,
No tear escapes the heart of You.
So take these worries, make them small,
And teach my heart to trust through all.

When doubt creeps in and shadows stay,
Remind me, Lord, to kneel and pray.
For peace begins where burdens end—
In hands of Christ, my dearest Friend.

Daily Reflection:
Casting Every Care

Promise Text: "Casting all your care upon Him; for He careth for you."
— 1 Peter 5:7

1. What specific worries or burdens am I holding onto right now that I need to release into God's hands? (Be honest—name them. The act of naming helps begin the letting go.)

2. How does knowing that God truly cares for me change the way I view my struggles, stress, or unanswered prayers? (Does it shift how I interpret delays, difficulties, or disappointments?)

3. What would "casting my care" look like in practice today? (A prayer? A journal entry? A conversation with someone I trust? What small step could I take to transfer my burdens to Him?)

Write your answers above or in a separate journal and date it with today's date. Now give and leave it with the Lord.

Day 12 - The Calm Within the Chaos

"Be careful for nothing; but in every thing by prayer and supplication with thanksgiving let your requests be made known unto God. And the peace of God, which passeth all understanding, shall keep your hearts and minds through Christ Jesus."
— Philippians 4:6–7

Peace is not found in the absence of problems but in the presence of prayer. Paul's command to *"be careful for nothing"* doesn't mean to stop caring—it means to stop carrying what only God can hold.

When we trade anxiety for gratitude, prayer becomes the bridge between worry and worship. The promise is not that all will go smoothly, but that God's peace—beyond comprehension—will guard our hearts and minds like a fortress. It's a peace that doesn't need explanations, because it's built on trust.

A modern-day example of this truth can be seen in Chesley "Sully" Sullenberger, the airline captain who safely landed US Airways Flight 1549 on the Hudson River after both engines failed.

In the minutes that followed the bird strike, 155 lives hung in the balance. Amid panic, Sully's calm demeanor became the difference between disaster and deliverance. Later, he said that years of preparation and presence of mind helped him act—but it was peace under pressure that carried him through.

That kind of inner stillness reflects the kind of peace God gives: not from training or talent alone, but from trust in something greater than fear.

When your life feels like it's losing altitude, remember—panic never saves, but prayer always steadies.

Bring your needs before God, thank Him even before the answer comes, and let His peace land gently in your soul. The world may not understand it, but Heaven guarantees it.

Peace That Guards My Soul

By Edward O. Anderson, Jr.
(Inspired by Philippians 4:6–7)

When fears arise and hearts lose ground,
Your peace, O Lord, is where I'm found.
No anxious thought, no sleepless night,
Can stand before Your calming light.

I'll bring my cares, both small and great,
And leave them at Your mercy's gate.
With thanks I'll rest, my mind made whole—
Your peace, my guard, my steady soul.

So when life shakes and tempests roll,
You'll be the anchor of my soul.
For prayer will rise where worries fall,
And Christ, my peace, will rule it all.

Daily Reflection:
The Calm Within the Chaos

Promise Text: "The peace of God, which passeth all understanding, shall keep your hearts and minds through Christ Jesus." — Philippians 4:7

1. What specific anxieties or situations have I been holding onto instead of releasing to God in prayer? (Be honest—naming your worries is the first step toward surrender.)

2. How would my daily outlook change if I approached every concern with gratitude instead of fear? (Gratitude shifts the heart from panic to perspective.)

3. Where have I seen God's peace carry me—or others—through moments that made no earthly sense? (Reflect on how divine calm has proven stronger than human control.)

Write your answers above or in a separate journal and date it with today's date. Now give and leave it with the Lord.

Day 13 - Grace for Today

"Take therefore no thought for the morrow: for the morrow shall take thought for the things of itself. Sufficient unto the day is the evil thereof."
— Matthew 6:34

Worry is the thief of today's peace and tomorrow's joy. Jesus' words remind us that God gives grace one day at a time—not in advance, but always on time. When we project our fears into the future, we step outside the place where His strength is present.

Christ's command is not to ignore responsibility, but to stop borrowing trouble from tomorrow. God hasn't promised to remove every storm, but He has promised enough grace for each day of it.

When you live one day at a time with Heaven's perspective, the weight of tomorrow begins to lose its hold.

One remarkable example of living this truth is Admiral James Stockdale, a U.S. Navy pilot who was shot down and held as a prisoner of war in Vietnam for over seven years. Tortured repeatedly and isolated from his fellow soldiers, Stockdale endured unimaginable conditions.

Later, when asked how he survived while others did not, he said, *"I never lost faith in the end of the story, but I also confronted the brutal facts of my current reality."* He lived one day at a time, trusting that endurance—one prayer, one breath, one decision at a time—would bring him through.

His steady faith and discipline mirror Jesus' call to focus on the grace given for today, not the fear of what's ahead.

When tomorrow feels uncertain and worry clouds your peace, remember: God is already in the future, but His strength is found here and now.

The same hand that holds your destiny holds your day. Live today fully, rest tonight deeply, and let tomorrow rest in God's capable hands.

Grace for Today

By Edward O. Anderson, Jr.
(Inspired by Matthew 6:34)

Lord, calm my mind, my racing heart,
From fears of days yet to start.
Teach me to trust what You provide,
Your daily grace, my faithful guide.

I'll rest in You and not in plans,
For all my days are in Your hands.
Today's enough—Your peace is near,
Tomorrow waits; I need not fear.

Each sunrise brings what You decree,
And every breath reminds of Thee.
So still my thoughts when doubts hold sway,
And help me live in grace for today.

Daily Reflection:
Grace for Today

Promise Text: "Take therefore no thought for the morrow..." — Matthew 6:34

1. What worries about tomorrow are stealing my peace today—and what would it look like to release them to God right now? (Be specific—naming them helps you hand them over.)

2. How has God faithfully provided for me one day at a time in the past? (Remembering His past provision renews confidence for the present.)

3. What small act of trust or gratitude can I practice today to keep my focus on God's present grace instead of future fears? (Living in the now opens space for peace to enter.)

Write your answers above or in a separate journal and date it with today's date. Now give and leave it with the Lord.

Day 14 - The Weight You Were Never Meant to Carry

*"Cast thy burden upon the Lord, and He shall sustain thee:
He shall never suffer the righteous to be moved."*
— Psalm 55:22

Life will hand you burdens too heavy for your shoulders. The psalmist knew this well—betrayal, fear, and pressure had driven him to his knees. Yet his answer wasn't to carry harder, but to cast quicker.

To "cast" means to throw off completely—to take what's crushing you and place it into the hands that never tremble.

God doesn't promise a life without burdens, but He does promise a shoulder that can sustain every one of them. The moment you let go, you find that peace is not the absence of problems—it's the presence of God's strength beneath them.

One powerful example of this truth comes from Harriet Tubman, the fearless leader of the Underground Railroad. Escaping slavery herself, she returned again and again to guide others to freedom—risking her life every time.

What few know is that Tubman often suffered from severe headaches and fainting spells due to a head injury, yet she never gave in to fear. She prayed before every rescue mission, saying, *"I always told God, I'm going to hold steady on You, and You've got to see me through."*

Each journey north was filled with danger, but she cast her burden on the Lord and found courage for what seemed impossible. Her trust turned fear into faith, and her faith set hundreds free.

When the load feels too much to bear—when you're weary, wounded, or weighed down—don't tighten your grip. Release it.

Throw it on the everlasting arms of God. You'll discover He doesn't just carry your burden—He carries you.

I Cast It All

By Edward O. Anderson., Jr.
(Inspired by Psalm 55:22)

The weight I hold, I lay it down,
Before Your cross, before Your crown.
My trembling hands release the care,
For You are strong enough to bear.

When worry shouts and peace feels small,
I'll cast, not cling—I'll give it all.
You lift the load, You calm the sea,
My burden's gone; You carry me.

Daily Reflection:
Casting the Weight

Promise Text: "Cast thy burden upon the Lord, and He shall sustain thee."
— Psalm 55:22

1. What burdens am I trying to carry on my own that God is inviting me to release today? (Be honest—naming them is the first act of surrender.)

2. How has God sustained me in the past when I chose to trust instead of control? (Remembering His past faithfulness strengthens your present confidence.)

3. What would it look like to cast—not just lay—my burden onto the Lord and truly leave it there? (Visualize yourself placing it in His hands and walking away in peace.)

Write your answers above or in a separate journal and date it with today's date. Now give and leave it with the Lord.

Day 15 - Perfect Peace in Imperfect Times

"Thou wilt keep him in perfect peace, whose mind is stayed on Thee: because he trusteth in Thee."
— Isaiah 26:3

Peace is not found in the absence of chaos but in the focus of the heart.

Isaiah reminds us that perfect peace—literally "peace, peace" in the Hebrew—belongs to those whose minds remain fixed on God, not their circumstances. The storms of life swirl around us, but when the eyes of faith stay locked on the Lord, the heart becomes steady.

The secret of peace is not control—it's trust. You cannot always still the winds, but you can choose where you anchor your thoughts. When you rest your mind on the One who never changes, His calm becomes your compass.

An inspiring example of this truth is Louis Zamperini, the World War II hero whose life was told in *Unbroken*. After surviving 47 days lost at sea and years of brutal imprisonment in a Japanese POW camp, Zamperini returned home tormented by anger and nightmares.

Peace eluded him until he attended a Billy Graham crusade in 1949. That night, he surrendered his pain to Christ—and found a supernatural peace that replaced years of rage.

From that moment forward, Louis forgave his captors and lived as a man transformed. He once said, *"I was not the same. My life was totally changed."* His story reminds us that when the mind is fixed on Christ, even the most shattered hearts can find rest.

You may not be able to control what comes against you, but you can choose where to place your focus.

Keep your thoughts anchored in God's promises, your faith steady in His character, and your heart will experience peace that defies logic and circumstance.

Perfect Peace

By Edward O. Anderson, Jr.
(Inspired by Isaiah 26:3)

Lord, still my mind when fears increase,
And fix my thoughts in perfect peace.
When chaos roars and shadows stay,
Teach me to trust, to rest, to pray.

You are the calm my heart has missed,
The peace that lives where faith persists.
No storm can steal what You impart,
When You, O Lord, guard mind and heart.

Daily Reflection:
Peace of Mind

Promise Text: "Thou wilt keep him in perfect peace, whose mind is stayed on Thee." — Isaiah 26:3

1. What thoughts or worries most often disturb my peace—and how can I redirect my focus toward God's promises instead? (Peace begins with what you choose to dwell on.)

2. When have I experienced peace that made no sense given my situation? (Remembering past peace builds faith for today's challenges.)

3. What practical steps can I take this week to "stay my mind" on God—through prayer, Scripture, or worship—when life feels out of control? (Peace is cultivated by consistency, not convenience.)

Write your answers above or in a separate journal and date it with today's date. Now give and leave it with the Lord.

When Darkness Seems Endless

The night may feel long, but morning always comes. God's light is not absent in the darkness — it is what the darkness cannot comprehend or extinguish.

Day 16 - Joy Comes in the Morning

*"For His anger endureth but a moment; in His favour is life:
weeping may endure for a night, but joy cometh in the morning."*
— Psalm 30:5

Every believer walks through nights of sorrow—seasons where God feels silent and hope seems dim. Yet David's psalm reminds us that no night lasts forever.

God's discipline or delay is momentary, but His favor is eternal. Grief may visit, but grace moves in to stay. The tears you shed today water the soil of tomorrow's joy.

Morning always follows midnight—not because the darkness isn't real, but because the light of God's mercy cannot be held back.

A powerful modern example of Psalm 30:5—*"Weeping may endure for a night, but joy cometh in the morning"*—is found in the story of Kurt Warner, the NFL quarterback who went from stocking grocery shelves to winning a Super Bowl.

After being cut from multiple teams and overlooked for years, Warner could have given up on his dream. Yet he held on to faith through every night of disappointment. When opportunity finally came with the St. Louis Rams, Warner not only led his team to a championship but also became one of the league's most inspiring figures.

He often spoke about how God used his struggles to strengthen his character and deepen his trust, saying, *"Sometimes you have to go through the darkness before you see the light."* His story is a living testimony that even when the night feels long, joy always comes in God's perfect timing.

You may be walking through a night of loss or disappointment, but take heart—God is not done writing your story. The night will end, and joy will rise again. Hold on to faith when the world is dark, for the morning light of His favor is already on its way.

Joy in the Morning

By Edward O. Anderson, Jr.
(Inspired by Psalm 30:5)

Lord, through the night when tears still fall,
Remind me You are over all.
Your mercy dawns with every sun,
And joy declares, "The night is done."

Though shadows linger, faith will stay,
For grace will greet the breaking day.
You turn my mourning into song—
Your joy shall lift me all life long.

Daily Reflection:
Joy After the Night

Promise Text: "Weeping may endure for a night, but joy cometh in the morning." — Psalm 30:5

1. What "night" am I currently walking through—and how can I remind myself that God's light is still coming? (Acknowledge the pain, but cling to His promise.)

2. Where in my past has God turned sorrow into joy or loss into growth? (Look back at how He's proven faithful through previous nights.)

3. What song of hope can I sing—literally or spiritually—while I wait for morning? (Joy begins in the heart before it breaks through the horizon.)

Write your answers above or in a separate journal and date it with today's date. Now give and leave it with the Lord.

Day 17 - Rising After the Fall

*"Rejoice not against me, O mine enemy: when I fall, I shall arise;
when I sit in darkness, the Lord shall be a light unto me."*
— Micah 7:8

Falling is not the end of your story—it's the beginning of your comeback.

Micah's words remind us that God's people may stumble, but they never stay down. The power of faith is not in avoiding failure, but in rising again through God's mercy.

Even when the night feels endless and shame whispers that it's over, the Lord Himself becomes your light. He shines not because you are perfect, but because He is faithful.

Every fall can be a classroom for grace, and every dark valley a place where His light becomes personal.

This truth echoes in the life of Walt Disney, who faced repeated failures before building one of the most influential creative empires in history. Early in his career, he was fired from a newspaper job for "lacking imagination." His first animation studio went bankrupt, and several of his ideas were rejected countless times.

Yet he refused to stay down. Disney once said, *"All the adversity I've had in my life, all my troubles and obstacles, have strengthened me."* What could have been the end of his dream became the soil for his greatest success.

Like Micah, Walt's story reminds us: failure is never final when you get up with faith.

So when you fall, rise. When you sit in darkness, look up.

The same God who spoke light into creation will speak hope into your soul. Let the enemy mock, let the critics whisper—but let faith answer: *"When I fall, I shall arise."*

I Shall Arise

By Edward O. Anderson, Jr.
(Inspired by Micah 7:8)

When darkness falls and hope seems small,
You lift me, Lord, above it all.
Though I may stumble, lose my way,
Your mercy greets each broken day.

You light the path when shadows grow,
You lift me up from depths below.
No fall too deep, no night too long,
For grace restores my heart with song.

So when I'm weak and dreams disguise,
Remind my soul—I shall arise.

Daily Reflection:
Rising Again

Promise Text: "When I fall, I shall arise; when I sit in darkness, the Lord shall be a light unto me." — Micah 7:8

1. Where in my life have I fallen or failed—and how can I allow God's light to turn that place into growth instead of guilt? (Failure is not final when surrendered to grace.)

2. Who or what has been trying to keep me down emotionally or spiritually— and how can I rise above it with God's help? (Identify your "enemy," then answer it with faith like Micah did.)

3. What would it look like for me to rise today, even in a small way—through forgiveness, courage, or renewed hope? (The first step up begins in the heart.)

Write your answers above or in a separate journal and date it with today's date. Now give and leave it with the Lord.

Day 18 - God Lights My Darkness

"For Thou wilt light my candle: the Lord my God will enlighten my darkness."
— Psalm 18:28

Darkness comes to every life—sometimes through grief, failure, confusion, or waiting. Yet David reminds us that we are never left without light.

God Himself becomes the flame that guides us through the shadows. When our strength fails, His presence ignites a flicker of faith; when our vision dims, His Word becomes the lamp for our feet.

The light of God doesn't always remove the darkness instantly—it teaches us how to walk through it one step at a time. What looks like the end of your story may simply be the beginning of God's illumination.

A powerful example of this truth is Johnny Cash, the legendary country musician who walked through deep valleys of addiction, depression, and self-destruction. At one of his lowest points, Cash crawled into a cave in Tennessee, intending never to return.

But in that moment of despair, he later recalled hearing God's voice reminding him that his life still had purpose. He stumbled back into the sunlight, choosing to live and trust again. That turning point reignited his faith, his music, and his mission.

Cash often testified that God's grace was the light that brought him out of the darkness. His comeback became one of the greatest redemption stories in music history.

When you can't see the way forward, remember: your darkness is not permanent, and your light is not gone—it's just hidden behind the clouds.

Let the Lord light your candle again. His flame is steady, His guidance sure, and His light will always lead you home.

Light My Candle, Lord

By Edward O. Anderson, Jr.

(Inspired by Psalm 18:28)

When night grows deep and hope feels small,
Lord, be the flame that warms it all.
Your light can pierce my darkest fear,
And whisper, "Child, I'm always near."

Though shadows hide the path ahead,
Your Word still shines where angels tread.
Light up my heart, renew my sight,
And guide me, Lord, through every night.

Daily Reflection:
Light in the Darkness

Promise Text: "For Thou wilt light my candle: the Lord my God will enlighten my darkness." — Psalm 18:28

1. What area of my life feels the darkest right now—and have I invited God's light to enter that place? (God can only light what you bring before Him.)

2. When has God illuminated my path in the past—guiding me through confusion, fear, or uncertainty? (Remembering past light rekindles present faith.)

3. What practical step can I take today to let God's light shine again in my thoughts, habits, or heart? (Even a small act of obedience can rekindle His flame.)

Write your answers above or in a separate journal and date it with today's date. Now give and leave it with the Lord.

Day 19 - The Light That Cannot Be Overcome

"And the light shineth in darkness; and the darkness comprehended it not."
— John 1:5

Light and darkness cannot coexist—when light appears, darkness must retreat.

John reminds us that Jesus is that eternal light, shining into the world's despair and the soul's deepest night. Darkness may try to surround you, but it can never extinguish the light of Christ. His presence doesn't just illuminate the path—it transforms the traveler.

Even when life feels clouded by loss, confusion, or sin, the light of Jesus keeps shining, guiding us toward hope and renewal. The darkness may linger, but it cannot win.

One person who lived this truth was Maya Angelou, the celebrated poet and author who endured a childhood marked by trauma, racism, and silence.

For years, she could not speak, believing her words had caused harm. Yet God's light reached into her silence and transformed it into strength. Through writing and faith, she found her voice again and went on to inspire millions with words of courage and healing.

Angelou once said, *"Nothing can dim the light which shines from within."* Her story is a powerful reflection of John's message: the light of God not only shines in the darkness—it shines through those who rise from it.

When your world feels dim, remember—the darkness doesn't get the final word. Christ's light is alive in you.

Let it burn brighter through prayer, kindness, and courage. The night cannot conquer the flame of faith that God has placed within your heart.

Shine Through Me

By Edward O. Anderson, Jr.
(Inspired by John 1:5)

When shadows fall and fears take hold,
Your light, O Lord, breaks strong and bold.
No night too deep, no wound too wide,
For still Your glory dwells inside.

Shine through my pain, my doubt, my fear,
Remind my heart that You are near.
The darkness flees—its power done,
For victory shines through Christ, the Son.

Daily Reflection:
Light That Lasts

Promise Text: "And the light shineth in darkness; and the darkness comprehended it not." — John 1:5

1. What "darkness" in my life is trying to overshadow my peace, and how can I let the light of Christ shine into that area today? (Darkness loses power when exposed to light.)

2. When has God's light guided me through confusion or fear in the past? (Remembering His past guidance strengthens faith in the present.)

3. How can I reflect Christ's light to someone who may be walking through their own darkness right now? (Every act of kindness becomes a beam of His presence.)

Write your answers above or in a separate journal and date it with today's date. Now give and leave it with the Lord.

Day 20 - Glory Beyond the Pain

*"For I reckon that the sufferings of this present time
are not worthy to be compared with the glory which shall be revealed in us."*
— Romans 8:18

Pain can make the world feel small and the future disappear, but Paul reminds us that our suffering—no matter how heavy—is temporary when viewed through eternity.

The storms of life are not wasted; they are shaping us for something greater. God doesn't minimize our pain, but He magnifies the purpose within it.

Every tear, every trial, every setback is part of a story that ends not in defeat, but in glory. What we see now is only the beginning of what God is preparing to reveal in and through us.

A powerful example of Romans 8:18 is seen in Serena Williams, one of the greatest tennis players in history. After giving birth in 2017, Serena suffered life-threatening complications that nearly ended her career—and her life.

Many doubted she could ever return to championship form. Yet through faith, discipline, and perseverance, she came back to compete at the highest level, reaching multiple Grand Slam finals while balancing motherhood and recovery. Serena once said, *"I've had setbacks before, and I've always used them as motivation to come back stronger."* Her journey reflects the truth that present suffering is never the end of the story for those who trust God's purpose.

The pain of today becomes the platform for tomorrow's glory, and the struggle of the moment is only the soil from which strength and victory grow.

When you're walking through hardship, remember that today's pain is not permanent—it's preparation.

The glory ahead will one day make every struggle worth it. Trust that what God is working in you is far greater than what the world can see right now.

The Glory Ahead

By Edward O. Anderson, Jr.
(Inspired by Romans 8:18)

When sorrow weighs upon my chest,
Remind me, Lord, Your plan is best.
The pain I feel is not the end—
It's shaping what You will defend.

Your glory waits beyond my tears,
Your promise stronger than my fears.
So help me walk this narrow way,
With hope that dawns a brighter day.

Daily Reflection:
The Purpose in the Pain

Promise Text: "The sufferings of this present time are not worthy to be compared with the glory which shall be revealed in us." — Romans 8:18

1. What hardship or disappointment am I facing right now that God may be using to build something deeper in me? (Suffering often reveals strength we didn't know we had.)

2. How has God already turned past pain into purpose in my life? (Looking back on His faithfulness gives courage to keep going.)

3. What future hope or promise from God can I focus on when the present feels heavy? (Shifting your view from pain to promise keeps your spirit lifted.)

Write your answers above or in a separate journal and date it with today's date. Now give and leave it with the Lord.

When You Need Faith to Keep Going

Faith isn't the absence of fear; it's the decision to keep walking when you can't see the road ahead. Every step of trust builds a bridge toward God's promise.

Day 21 - Faith When You Can't See

*"Now faith is the substance of things hoped for,
the evidence of things not seen."*
— Hebrews 11:1

Faith is trusting God when the map is missing and the fog is thick.

It is believing His promises even when you can't see His plan.

The writer of Hebrews reminds us that faith isn't wishful thinking—it's confidence in God's unseen reality. Faith gives substance to hope, turning what we cannot see into what we can stand on.

Every step of faith may feel risky, but it's never reckless when your trust is anchored in the One who never fails.

A remarkable example of living by faith is Colonel Gail Halvorsen, known as "The Candy Bomber" during the Berlin Airlift after World War II.

Surrounded by the devastation of war, Halvorsen was moved by the sight of hungry German children watching Allied planes deliver supplies. He decided to drop small parachutes of candy for them, using his own rations.

What began as a simple act of kindness became a global symbol of hope. He couldn't see how far one small gesture would reach, but he believed that light could pierce darkness. His faith in goodness—and in God's ability to work through compassion—lifted an entire generation out of despair.

When the path ahead is uncertain, hold onto the faith that sees beyond sight.

You may not know how God will work, but you can trust that He will. Faith isn't about knowing the outcome—it's about knowing the One who holds it.

Eyes of Faith

By Edward O. Anderson, Jr.
(Inspired by Hebrews 11:1)

When shadows hide what lies ahead,
I'll trust the words that You have said.
Though I can't see, I'll still believe,
For faith is sight I can't perceive.

You speak, and hope begins to grow,
Your unseen hand still leads me so.
Through every doubt, my heart will stay,
For faith walks strong where eyes give way.

Daily Reflection:
Faith That Sees the Unseen

Promise Text: "Faith is the substance of things hoped for, the evidence of things not seen." — Hebrews 11:1

1. What situation in my life right now requires me to trust God even though I can't see how it will work out? (Faith begins where sight ends.)

2. When has God proven faithful in the past after I took a step of faith? (Remembering past victories fuels courage for the present.)

3. What act of faith—small or great—is God asking me to take today? (Faith grows stronger through action, not just belief.)

Write your answers above or in a separate journal and date it with today's date. Now give and leave it with the Lord.

Day 22 - Walking by Faith, Not by Sight

"For we walk by faith, not by sight."
— 2 Corinthians 5:7

Walking by faith means moving forward even when you can't see the full path ahead. It's trusting God's direction when the destination is still hidden.

Faith doesn't deny reality—it simply believes that God's reality is greater than what we can see. Paul's words remind us that faith is a journey, not a moment.

Sometimes, the road will twist through uncertainty, pain, or delay, but faith keeps walking because it knows the One leading the way. Sight can fail; faith never does when it's fixed on Jesus.

A vivid example of this kind of faith is Harriet Beecher Stowe, author of Uncle Tom's Cabin. In a time of fierce racial division and political danger, she felt God call her to expose the sin of slavery through her writing.

Despite fear, threats, and financial hardship, she obeyed that call. Her book ignited national debate and stirred hearts across the world.

President Abraham Lincoln reportedly greeted her by saying, *"So you're the little woman who wrote the book that started this great war."* Stowe didn't know how God would use her obedience—she simply walked by faith, one word at a time. Through her courage, countless lives and hearts were changed.

When you cannot see what's next, remember: your faith walk is not about the size of your steps, but the certainty of your Guide.

Keep walking, even in the dark, for God's path often becomes clearest in the moments you choose to trust Him most.

The Faithful Path

By Edward O. Anderson, Jr,
(Inspired by 2 Corinthians 5:7)

Lord, when the road is dark and long,
And courage fades where fears belong,
Remind my heart to trust, not see,
For every step is led by Thee.

Though sight may fail and doubt draws near,
Your whispered truth still calms my fear.
Each step I take, Your hand will guide,
By faith, not sight, I'll walk beside.

Daily Reflection:
The Journey of Trust

Promise Text: "For we walk by faith, not by sight." — 2 Corinthians 5:7

1. Where in my life am I waiting to "see" before I trust—and what would it look like to take one step of faith instead? (Faith grows stronger when exercised, not when explained.)

2. How has God proven Himself trustworthy in times when I didn't know how things would turn out? (Remembering past faithfulness builds courage for the next step.)

3. What small act of obedience is God calling me to take today that requires faith, not sight? (Faith in motion becomes testimony in time.)

Write your answers above or in a separate journal and date it with today's date. Now give and leave it with the Lord.

Day 23 - Joy in the Testing

"My brethren, count it all joy when ye fall into divers temptations;
knowing this, that the trying of your faith worketh patience.
But let patience have her perfect work, that ye may be perfect and entire,
wanting nothing." — James 1:2–4

Trials don't come to destroy you—they come to develop you.

James calls us to see hardship through Heaven's eyes: not as punishment, but as preparation. The testing of your faith is the training ground for spiritual endurance.

Joy in trials doesn't mean pretending the pain isn't real; it means believing that God is doing something real through it. Each struggle refines your patience, deepens your character, and strengthens your trust in God.

Faith that's never tested remains shallow—but faith that endures becomes unshakable.

A living example of this is Joni Eareckson Tada, who at age 17 became a quadriplegic after a diving accident. Her early years after the accident were filled with despair and anger, but as she turned to God, her suffering became the soil for a deeper faith.

Over time, Joni learned to paint with her mouth, write best-selling books, and found Joni and Friends, a global ministry serving people with disabilities. She once said, *"The weaker I am, the harder I must lean on God's grace, and the stronger I discover Him to be."* Her joy was not the denial of pain—it was the triumph of trust.

Joni's endurance became her testimony, proving that God can turn tragedy into triumph and testing into transformation.

Your current trial may feel like a fire, but it's refining gold within you. Don't rush what God is building.

Let patience finish her work, for when she does, you will emerge stronger, steadier, and filled with joy that no storm can steal.

Joy in the Fire

By Edward O. Anderson, Jr.
(Inspired by James 1:2–4)

When troubles rise and faith feels small,
Lord, help me trust You through it all.
Each test I face, each tear I cry,
Becomes the place where faith will fly.

Teach me to see beyond the pain,
To find the joy that still remains.
Your hand refines, Your love restores—
Through every trial, my heart endures.

Daily Reflection:
Strength in the Struggle

Promise Text: "Count it all joy when ye fall into divers temptations…" — James 1:2–4

1. What current trial in my life might God be using to strengthen my patience and deepen my faith? (Endurance grows only through experience.)

2. When has God turned a past hardship into something that later produced blessing or growth? (Looking back reveals His faithfulness.)

3. How can I shift my perspective today from frustration to faith, seeing this test as preparation instead of punishment? (Joy begins when we trust the purpose behind the pain.)

Write your answers above or in a separate journal and date it with today's date. Now give and leave it with the Lord.

Day 24 - Hope That Does Not Disappoint

*"And not only so, but we glory in tribulations also:
knowing that tribulation worketh patience;
and patience, experience; and experience, hope: and hope maketh not ashamed;
because the love of God is shed abroad in our hearts
by the Holy Ghost which is given unto us."*
— Romans 5:3–5

Pain is never pleasant, but in God's hands, it becomes powerful. Paul teaches that suffering is not meaningless—it is the soil where endurance grows, and endurance produces character that blossoms into hope.

This is not the kind of hope that fades with disappointment, but one anchored in the unchanging love of God. When life breaks you down, faith builds you up. Every hardship that seems to crush you is secretly preparing you for something eternal.

The presence of pain doesn't mean the absence of God—it's often the place where His love is most deeply revealed.

A shining example of this truth is Viktor Frankl, an Austrian psychiatrist and Holocaust survivor. While imprisoned in Nazi concentration camps, Frankl lost his family, his freedom, and everything familiar. Yet in that horror, he discovered an enduring truth: though he could not control his circumstances, he could control his response.

Out of unimaginable suffering came his book *Man's Search for Meaning*, in which he wrote, "*When we are no longer able to change a situation, we are challenged to change ourselves.*" Frankl found that hope, rooted in purpose, could survive even the darkest night. His life is a testimony that tribulation can refine the soul and lead to unshakable faith in what truly matters.

When trials press in, remember that God's love is still at work within you. Endurance is being formed. Character is being shaped. And hope is being born.

The storm may last for a night, but the sunrise of God's promise is certain.

Hope Through the Fire

By Edward O. Anderson, Jr.
(Inspired by Romans 5:3–5)

When trials come and shadows stay,
Lord, teach my heart to trust Your way.
Through pain and fire, Your love refines,
And hope eternal in me shines.

Though tears may fall and nights feel long,
Your Spirit fills my soul with song.
For every trial, You turn to grace—
And hope still blooms in darkened place.

Daily Reflection:
Strength That Builds Hope

Promise Text: "Tribulation worketh patience; and patience, experience; and experience, hope." — Romans 5:3–5

1. What current challenge is God using to build patience and strengthen my character? (Ask Him to show you what He's forming through this season.)

2. When has endurance in the past led to deeper hope and trust in God's faithfulness? (Reflect on how pain has produced spiritual growth before.)

3. How can I let God's love shape my attitude during times of suffering rather than letting bitterness take root? (Remember—hope grows best in hearts watered by love.)

Write your answers above or in a separate journal and date it with today's date. Now give and leave it with the Lord.

Day 25 - Wait With Courage

"I had fainted, unless I had believed to see the goodness of the Lord in the land of the living. Wait on the Lord: be of good courage, and He shall strengthen thine heart: wait, I say, on the Lord." — Psalm 27:13–14

Faith isn't tested in moments of comfort—it's tested in the waiting room of uncertainty.

David confessed that he would have lost heart unless he believed he would see God's goodness. The key word is believed. Waiting is not passive; it's an act of faith. When we trust God's timing, even in seasons of silence or delay, we are strengthened from within.

The waiting is where God prepares both the promise and the person. And in the end, those who wait in hope never wait in vain.

A shining example of Psalm 27:13–14 is found in Simone Biles, the legendary Olympic gymnast. After facing years of grueling training, mental pressure, and even stepping back during the 2021 Tokyo Olympics to protect her mental health, Simone had to wait patiently for her moment of restoration.

Many questioned whether she would ever return to competition, but through courage, faith, and perseverance, she did. In 2023, Biles made a remarkable comeback, reclaiming her place atop the world stage and winning gold again. She later shared, *"I had to trust the process, give myself grace, and wait until I was ready."* Her journey is a powerful reminder that waiting is not weakness—it's strength under control.

Like David, Simone's story proves that those who wait on the Lord with courage and faith will indeed see His goodness break through in due time.

When it feels like your prayers are unanswered or your breakthrough is delayed, take heart. God's timeline is not denial—it's preparation.

The strength you gain while waiting will become the faith you stand on when the promise arrives.

Strength in the Waiting

By Edward O. Anderson, Jr.
(Inspired by Psalm 27:13–14)

When hope feels faint and nights are long,
Lord, be my heart, my steady song.
Though I can't see, I'll stand and stay,
For You are near in every delay.

Give courage, Lord, to trust Your hand,
Though I can't yet see where I'll stand.
You strengthen hearts that wait and pray—
So teach me, Lord, to wait Your way.

Daily Reflection:
Courage While You Wait

Promise Text: "Wait on the Lord: be of good courage, and He shall strengthen thine heart." — Psalm 27:14

1. Where in my life right now do I feel tempted to give up instead of waiting on God's timing? (Identify the area where faith is being tested.)

2. How has waiting in past seasons actually strengthened me rather than weakened me? (Remember how endurance builds faith.)

3. What would it look like to "wait with courage" today instead of waiting with fear or frustration? (Patience with purpose turns waiting into worship.)

Write your answers above or in a separate journal and date it with today's date. Now give and leave it with the Lord.

When You Feel Alone

Loneliness lies — you are never truly alone. The same God who parts seas and moves mountains also sits beside you in silence and whispers, "I am still here."

Day 26 - You Are Not Alone

"And the Lord, He it is that doth go before thee;
He will be with thee, He will not fail thee, neither forsake thee:
fear not, neither be dismayed."
— Deuteronomy 31:8

Loneliness often arrives before great transitions—when you step into the unknown, face a challenge, or walk through loss. God gave this promise to Joshua as he prepared to lead Israel into the Promised Land: *"You are not alone."* It wasn't a command to be fearless—it was a reminder of God's presence.

When fear whispers that you're unqualified or forgotten, faith must answer with the truth that the Lord has already gone before you. He walks ahead to prepare the way, beside you to guide the steps, and behind you to protect your back. The journey may feel uncertain, but His presence is unshakable.

A powerful modern example of Deuteronomy 31:8 is found in Admiral William H. McRaven, the U.S. Navy SEAL who led the operation that brought down Osama bin Laden.

Throughout his decades of service, McRaven faced immense danger, uncertainty, and moments where failure seemed certain. Yet his leadership under fire was marked by courage, calm, and conviction that the mission was greater than the man.

In his now-famous commencement speech, he said, *"If you want to change the world, start by making your bed."* His words reflected a deeper truth—that courage begins with discipline, faith, and trust that God is ahead of every battle. McRaven's life illustrates the heart of Deuteronomy 31:8: no matter the danger, when you trust that the Lord has gone before you, you can stand firm and move forward without fear.

When fear grips your heart or the road ahead seems too great to face, remember this—God hasn't abandoned you.

He is already in your tomorrow, clearing the obstacles you can't yet see. So walk forward with confidence: you never walk alone.

Never Alone

By Edward O. Anderson, Jr.
(Inspired by Deuteronomy 31:8)

When fear draws near and shadows stay,
Remind me, Lord, You've led the way.
Before I move, You've gone ahead,
My steps are guided where You've led.

You'll never leave, nor turn aside,
Your presence, Lord, will be my guide.
Though I can't see what waits unknown,
I'll walk by faith—I'm not alone.

Daily Reflection:
The God Who Goes Before You

Promise Text: "He will be with thee; He will not fail thee, neither forsake thee." — Deuteronomy 31:8

1. What situation in my life right now feels uncertain or intimidating, and how can I remind myself that God has already gone before me? (Faith begins by remembering He's already there.)

2. When has God proven His presence and faithfulness in past moments of fear or change? (Look back on times when His guidance carried you.)

3. What practical step of courage can I take today because I know I am not alone? (Courage grows when we act on His promises, not our fears.)

Write your answers above or in a separate journal and date it with today's date. Now give and leave it with the Lord.

Day 27 - Never Alone in the Mission

"Lo, I am with you always, even unto the end of the world.
— Matthew 28:20

When Jesus gave the Great Commission, He didn't just give a mission—He gave a promise. *"I am with you always."* Those words anchor the heart in every season of life—when the task feels too large, the fear too strong, or the night too long.

Jesus didn't promise a storm-free journey, but He did promise His unbroken presence through it all. Wherever you go and whatever you face, He walks beside you. Even when you feel unseen or overwhelmed, His Spirit is nearer than your breath.

Faith isn't about walking perfectly—it's about walking with Him.

A profound example of Matthew 28:20 is found in Mother Teresa, the humble servant of God who dedicated her life to caring for the poorest of the poor in Calcutta. Surrounded by suffering, disease, and death, she often worked in places where few dared to go. Yet her courage came not from her own strength, but from her unwavering belief in Christ's presence beside her.

Even in her private writings, where she confessed seasons of spiritual dryness, she never stopped serving—trusting that Jesus was still near, even when she couldn't feel Him. Mother Teresa once said, *"I know God won't give me anything I can't handle. I just wish He didn't trust me so much."* Through exhaustion and loneliness, she carried the light of Christ into the darkest corners of the world. Her life reminds us that God's presence is not confined to comfort— it shines most brightly in the places of deepest need, where love and faith meet extraordinary courage.

When you walk through difficulty or face daunting purpose, remember— God never sends you alone. He is in the conversation, in the crisis, in the calling. The world may shift, but His presence never leaves.

The One who began the journey with you will finish it by your side.

You Are With Me Always

By Edward O. Anderson, Jr.
(Inspired by Matthew 28:20)

When courage fades and strength feels small,
You whisper, "Child, I'm through it all."
Through fear and fire, storm and strain,
Your presence stays, my heart's refrain.

You go before, You stand behind,
In every season, peace I find.
Though worlds may end and time may flee,
Forever, Lord, You walk with me.

Daily Reflection:
His Presence in Every Place

Promise Text: "Lo, I am with you always, even unto the end of the world."
— Matthew 28:20

1. Where in my life do I most need to remember that Jesus is with me right now? (His presence is constant, even when unseen.)

2. How has God's presence carried me through moments when I felt abandoned or overwhelmed? (Look back to see how His promise has proven true.)

3. What would change in my attitude or courage if I truly lived with the awareness that Jesus walks beside me every moment? (Faith grows stronger when you practice His presence daily.)

Write your answers above or in a separate journal and date it with today's date. Now give and leave it with the Lord.

Day 28 - God's Presence in Every Place

"Whither shall I go from Thy Spirit? or whither shall I flee from Thy presence?
If I ascend up into heaven, Thou art there:
if I make my bed in hell, behold, Thou art there.
If I take the wings of the morning, and dwell in the uttermost parts of the sea;
even there shall Thy hand lead me, and Thy right hand shall hold me."
— Psalm 139:7–10

There is no place you can go where God's presence cannot reach you.

David discovered this truth in his darkest and brightest moments alike. Whether he was on the throne or in the cave, God was there. His Spirit does not depend on our surroundings or emotions—it is constant, unshakable, and deeply personal.

Sometimes we try to outrun our pain or escape our failures, but even there, His mercy meets us. The One who fills the heavens also fills the heart that feels alone. His hand is not just near—it's guiding, holding, and lifting us through every storm.

A powerful modern example of this truth is Desmond Doss, the World War II combat medic portrayed in Hacksaw Ridge. A man of faith who refused to carry a weapon, Doss faced persecution from his own unit and unimaginable danger on the battlefield. Yet during the Battle of Okinawa, when the gunfire roared and fear surrounded him, he prayed, *"Lord, help me get one more."*

That night, he rescued 75 soldiers single-handedly under fire. Doss later said he never felt alone—he knew God's hand was guiding him. His courage came not from absence of fear, but from the awareness of divine presence in the very center of chaos.

No matter where you are—on the mountaintop of victory or the valley of despair—God is there. His presence fills your silence, steadies your steps, and strengthens your soul.

You may feel far from peace, but you're never far from Him.

Even There

By Edward O. Anderson, Jr.
(Inspired by Psalm 139:7–10)

When darkness hides Your gentle face,
I know You're here, still full of grace.
From sky to sea, from fear to prayer,
No place exists where You're not there.

Your hand will guide, Your love will stay,
Through every night and dawning day.
Though I may fall, though paths may tear,
You lift me up—for You are there.

Daily Reflection:
His Presence Never Fails

Promise Text: "Even there shall Thy hand lead me, and Thy right hand shall hold me." — Psalm 139:10

1. Where in my life have I felt distant from God—and how can I remind myself that His presence is still near? (Feelings fade, but His promise stands.)

2. When has God's hand guided me through a place I didn't think I'd survive? (Remembering past guidance renews present trust.)

3. What practical way can I invite greater awareness of God's presence today—through prayer, worship, or gratitude? (Peace begins when you recognize you are never alone.)

Write your answers above or in a separate journal and date it with today's date. Now give and leave it with the Lord.

Day 29 - Unbreakable Love

"For I am persuaded, that neither death, nor life, nor angels, nor principalities,
nor powers, nor things present, nor things to come, nor height, nor depth,
nor any other creature, shall be able to separate us from the love of God,
which is in Christ Jesus our Lord."
— Romans 8:38–39

Paul's conviction is bold and immovable—nothing can separate us from God's love. Not tragedy, not failure, not fear, and not even death itself. His love is not conditional; it is constant, unbreakable, and eternal.

When storms rise and hearts break, His love does not waver—it reaches deeper. The same love that reached Paul in prison reaches us in our darkest valleys. You may lose strength, peace, or people—but never His love.

When you are too weak to hold on to God, He holds on to you.

A powerful example of Romans 8:38–39 is seen in the life of Billy Graham, one of the most influential evangelists of all time. Throughout his decades of ministry, Billy faced opposition, illness, criticism, and personal loss, yet he remained steadfast in his faith that nothing could separate him—or anyone—from the love of God.

He preached to over 200 million people across nearly every nation, always pointing hearts back to the unbreakable love of Christ. Even near the end of his life, when frailty and blindness set in, Graham declared, *"I'm not afraid to die, for I know the joys of heaven are waiting."* His unwavering trust in God's love through every season of triumph and trial stands as a living testimony that divine love is stronger than fear, failure, or even death itself.

Billy Graham's legacy reminds us that no matter where we go or what we face, God's love never lets go—it carries us all the way home.

When you feel forgotten or unloved, remember—God's love is not a feeling; it is a fact. It surrounds you, sustains you, and will never let you go.

Even when life seems against you, His love remains for you.

Held by Love

By Edward O. Anderson, Jr.
(Inspired by Romans 8:38–39)

When shadows fall and doubts arise,
Your love still shines through clouded skies.
No height, no depth, no night, no pain,
Can steal the love that will remain.

You've held me close through storm and fire,
Your love unending, lifting higher.
Though all may change, Your Word is true—
Forever, Lord, I'm bound to You.

Daily Reflection:
Anchored in His Love

Promise Text: "Nothing shall be able to separate us from the love of God."
— Romans 8:39

1. What current struggle makes me feel distant from God—and how can I remind myself that His love has never left me? (Feelings change, but His love never does.)

2. When has God's love sustained me through a storm that should have broken me? (Reflect on how His presence carried you when you couldn't stand.)

3. How can I reflect God's unstoppable love toward someone else who feels unworthy or forgotten today? (Love shared is love strengthened.)

Write your answers above or in a separate journal and date it with today's date. Now give and leave it with the Lord.

Day 30 - Be Strong and Courageous

"Have not I commanded thee? Be strong and of a good courage;
be not afraid, neither be thou dismayed:
for the Lord thy God is with thee whithersoever thou goest."
— *Joshua 1:9*

When Joshua faced the daunting task of leading Israel into the Promised Land, fear could have easily paralyzed him. But God's command was clear—be strong and courageous. This wasn't a call to self-confidence; it was a call to God-confidence.

True courage doesn't come from the absence of fear but from the assurance of God's presence.

When you know the Lord goes with you, you can face whatever lies ahead—uncertain seasons, new callings, or unexpected storms—with steady faith and quiet strength.

A powerful illustration of this courage can be seen in Rosa Parks, whose simple act of defiance sparked a movement that changed history.

On December 1, 1955, Parks refused to give up her seat on a Montgomery bus, fully aware of the danger and backlash she would face. Later, she said, *"I have learned over the years that when one's mind is made up, this diminishes fear."* Her bravery didn't come from her own strength—it came from a conviction that what she stood for was right and that God would stand with her.

Like Joshua, she moved forward in faith, knowing that divine courage always overcomes human fear.

When life calls you to take a stand or step into something new, remember—courage is not the absence of trembling knees; it's trusting that the Lord walks beside you every step of the way.

You don't go alone.

Courage to Stand

By Edward O. Anderson, Jr.
(Inspired by Joshua 1:9)

When fear would rise and shadows fall,
You whisper, "Child, I'm over all."
Through trials deep, through nights so long,
Your presence keeps my spirit strong.

So give me faith, though storms may rage,
To walk with You on every stage.
For where You lead, I will not flee—
My courage lives because of Thee.

Daily Reflection:
Strength for the Journey

Promise Text: "Be strong and of a good courage… for the Lord thy God is with thee whithersoever thou goest." — Joshua 1:9

1. What situation am I facing right now that requires me to be strong and courageous in faith? (Name the challenge and bring it before the Lord.)

2. How has God's presence sustained me through fearful or uncertain times before?(Remembering past faithfulness renews present confidence.)

3. What small step of obedience can I take today to show courage in action, not just in words? (Courage grows with every act of trust.)

Write your answers above or in a separate journal and date it with today's date. Now give and leave it with the Lord.

When You Need to Remember God's Power

Storms may roar, but God still reigns. His hand is not shortened; His strength has not faded. The same power that spoke the universe into being now fights for you.

Day 31 - The Lord Will Fight for You

"The Lord shall fight for you, and ye shall hold your peace."
— *Exodus 14:14*

When Israel stood at the edge of the Red Sea with Pharaoh's army closing in, fear took hold. The people saw no way out—but God saw a way through. Moses spoke these powerful words: *"The Lord shall fight for you."*

It was a reminder that victory doesn't depend on our strength but on God's sovereignty. Sometimes God calls us to move; other times He calls us to be still and trust. Peace doesn't come from escaping the battle, but from knowing who fights beside—and before—you.

When we let go of control, we make room for God to do the impossible.

A powerful example of this truth can be seen in Dietrich Bonhoeffer, the German pastor and theologian who stood against the Nazi regime during World War II.

Imprisoned for his faith and ultimately executed for resisting evil, Bonhoeffer faced darkness with unshakable peace. From his prison cell, he wrote, *"We must be ready to allow ourselves to be interrupted by God."* He trusted that even in captivity, God was fighting the greater battle for truth and justice.

Bonhoeffer's courage reminds us that holding our peace doesn't mean doing nothing—it means resting in the confidence that God is working, even when we cannot see how.

When you feel surrounded by impossible odds, remember this: the same God who parted the Red Sea still parts the seas in your life.

Stand still, trust deeply, and watch Him make a way where there seems to be none.

The Battle Is Yours

By Edward O. Anderson, Jr.
(Inspired by Exodus 14:14)

When fears press in and strength feels small,
Lord, teach me You are over all.
Though storms surround and doubts may rise,
Your hand still fights—my heart relies.

I'll hold my peace, I'll stand and see,
The battles won belong to Thee.
Through faith, I'll wait, through grace, I'll stay—
For You will make a mighty way.

Daily Reflection:
Standing Still in Faith

Promise Text: "The Lord shall fight for you, and ye shall hold your peace."
— Exodus 14:14

1. What battle am I facing today that feels too great for me to handle? (Name it—and remember, it's not too great for God.)

2. How can I "hold my peace" and choose trust over panic in this situation? (Stillness often allows God's strength to shine.)

3. When has God fought for me in the past and proven His faithfulness? (Looking back reminds your heart that He'll do it again.)

Write your answers above or in a separate journal and date it with today's date. Now give and leave it with the Lord.

Day 32 - When He Calms the Storm

"He maketh the storm a calm, so that the waves thereof are still."
— Psalm 107:29

Life's storms can come suddenly—an illness, loss, or crisis that shakes our confidence and drowns our peace. But the same God who calmed the seas for the disciples still speaks peace into the waves of our hearts.

The psalmist reminds us that God's power extends not just over the physical elements but over the emotional and spiritual tempests that threaten to overwhelm us. When we call upon Him, He doesn't always stop the storm immediately, but He always calms the soul within it.

His peace is not the absence of chaos—it's the presence of Christ in the middle of it.

One remarkable story of faith through the storm is that of Captain Eddie Rickenbacker, a World War I flying ace who later survived 24 days adrift in the Pacific Ocean during World War II after his plane went down.

With no food, limited water, and the scorching sun, Rickenbacker and his crew fought despair daily. Yet they prayed and trusted that God would deliver them. One day, a seagull landed on his head—miraculously becoming their food and bait for fish, keeping them alive until rescue.

Rickenbacker later said, *"The most important thing in a storm is that you pray."* His experience became a living testimony that even in life's fiercest storms, God can bring stillness and supply from the most unexpected places.

Your storm may roar and your boat may shake, but God's Word still commands the wind.

When the waves rise, remember—the calm is coming, and the One who holds the ocean also holds you.

Peace in the Waves

By Edward O. Anderson, Jr.
(Inspired by Psalm 107:29)

When waves arise and tempests roar,
Lord, calm my heart, I ask no more.
You speak, and winds obey Your will,
The storm grows quiet, the sea grows still.

Through every trial, fierce and long,
You are my peace, my anchor strong.
So when I fear or faith feels small,
Remind my soul—You rule it all.

Daily Reflection:
Finding Calm in the Chaos

Promise Text: "He maketh the storm a calm, so that the waves thereof are still." — Psalm 107:29

1. What "storm" in my life right now is threatening my peace, and how can I invite God to speak calm into it? (Naming the storm helps you release it into His control.)

2. When has God calmed a storm in my past—spiritually, emotionally, or physically? (Remembering past peace renews present trust.)

3. What might God be teaching me in the middle of this current storm that I couldn't learn in calm waters? (Even storms have purpose when guided by His hand.)

Write your answers above or in a separate journal and date it with today's date. Now give and leave it with the Lord.

Day 33 - Safe in the Storm

**"The Lord is good, a strong hold in the day of trouble;
and He knoweth them that trust in Him."
— Nahum 1:7**

Nahum's words remind us that God's goodness isn't limited to peaceful seasons—He is good in the storm, not just after it. When everything feels uncertain, He remains a strong and steady refuge.

God doesn't just provide shelter; He is the shelter. He personally knows those who trust Him—every tear, every cry, every moment of silent endurance. The storms of life may rage, but His goodness is immovable.

He may not always calm the wind right away, but He always covers His children in the midst of it.

A powerful example of Nahum 1:7 is found in Malala Yousafzai, the young Pakistani activist who stood fearlessly for girls' education in the face of violent oppression.

At just fifteen years old, Malala was targeted and shot by the Taliban for speaking out against their restrictions on women's rights. Her body was broken, but her spirit was unshaken. Through her long recovery, she leaned on her faith and inner conviction that God had preserved her life for a purpose. Malala later said, *"They thought the bullets would silence us, but they failed."* Instead, her voice grew stronger, reaching the world as a message of courage, forgiveness, and hope. Her life is a living portrait of Nahum 1:7—when darkness pressed in, she found refuge in God's strength.

Malala's unwavering stand reminds us that even when we feel alone in our battle for truth or justice, God Himself stands beside those who trust in Him.

When fear surrounds you, take refuge in the One who knows you by name.

You don't have to stand strong on your own—your strength is found in the goodness of God, who will never fail those who trust Him.

My Refuge and My Rest

By Edward O. Anderson, Jr.
(Inspired by Nahum 1:7)

When trials rise and shadows stay,
Lord, be my strength, my rock, my way.
Your goodness stands when all else falls,
A refuge strong through life's great calls.

You know my heart, You hear my plea,
No safer place than close to Thee.
Through every storm, through every test,
I'll trust Your name—my peace, my rest.

Daily Reflection:
Trusting in His Goodness

Promise Text: "The Lord is good, a strong hold in the day of trouble; and He knoweth them that trust in Him." — Nahum 1:7

1. Where do I need to run to God for refuge today instead of trying to handle things on my own? (True strength begins in surrender.)

2. How has God proven His goodness to me in past seasons of trouble? (Remembering past protection builds present peace.)

3. What does trusting God look like for me right now—emotionally, spiritually, or practically? (Faith in action brings peace in motion.)

Write your answers above or in a separate journal and date it with today's date. Now give and leave it with the Lord.

Day 34 - Beyond What You Can Imagine

"Now unto Him that is able to do exceeding abundantly above all that we ask or think, according to the power that worketh in us."
— *Ephesians 3:20*

God's power is not limited by our expectations.

He doesn't just meet needs—He multiplies miracles. Paul reminds us that God can do exceeding abundantly more than we can ask or even imagine.

Often, our prayers are too small because we measure God's ability by our own limitations. But faith invites us to dream beyond the visible, to trust that the same power that raised Christ from the dead is at work within us.

When life closes one door, God is already preparing another—bigger, better, and far beyond our understanding.

A living example of this verse is Oprah Winfrey. Born into poverty and faced with abuse, rejection, and discrimination, she could have let her circumstances define her. Instead, she dared to believe that her life had purpose.

Through perseverance, faith, and vision, Oprah rose from obscurity to become one of the most influential women in the world. She has often credited her faith as the foundation of her journey, saying, *"God can dream a bigger dream for you than you could ever dream for yourself."*

Her story reflects the truth that God can turn hardship into hope and pain into purpose—doing more than we could ever plan when we surrender our plans to Him.

Whatever you're praying for today, remember: God's vision for your life far exceeds your imagination.

When you feel like you've reached your limit, that's where His abundance begins.

More Than Enough

By Edward O. Anderson, Jr.
(Inspired by Ephesians 3:20)

Lord, lift my faith beyond my view,
To dream the dreams designed by You.
When I see little, You see grand,
Your mighty work is in Your hand.

Do more than I could ever ask,
Through every trial, through every task.
Your power lives and moves in me,
Unfolding grace abundantly.

Daily Reflection:
Believing for More

Promise Text: "Now unto Him that is able to do exceeding abundantly above all that we ask or think." — Ephesians 3:20

1. What prayer or dream have I limited because I assumed it was too big or impossible? (God's power begins where your limits end.)

2. When has God surprised me by doing more than I expected or prayed for? (Gratitude fuels greater faith.)

3. How can I align my prayers today with God's abundance instead of my own limitations? (Faith asks boldly and trusts fully.)

Write your answers above or in a separate journal and date it with today's date. Now give and leave it with the Lord.

Day 35 - Nothing Is Too Hard for God

"Behold, I am the Lord, the God of all flesh:
is there any thing too hard for Me?"
— Jeremiah 32:27

When Jeremiah heard God ask this question, he was imprisoned and Jerusalem was under siege. From a human perspective, everything looked impossible—defeat seemed certain. Yet God reminded him that His power is not limited by circumstances.

What looks hopeless to us is still within the realm of God's control. Faith is not denying reality—it's believing that God is greater than reality.

The same voice that created the world with a word can speak life into your situation. There is no sickness too severe, no door too closed, no heart too hard, and no dream too far gone for the Lord of all flesh.

A striking modern example is Elon Musk, founder of SpaceX and Tesla. Before he became a symbol of innovation, Musk nearly lost everything—Tesla was on the brink of bankruptcy, SpaceX's first three rocket launches failed, and critics mocked his vision.

Yet Musk persisted when failure seemed inevitable. On the fourth launch, the rocket succeeded, saving both companies. While his success is rooted in determination and not specifically faith, his story reflects a powerful truth: the human spirit can persevere when it believes in what seems impossible.

For the believer, how much more when we place our trust not in our own strength, but in the limitless power of God?

When life corners you and hope feels distant, listen again to God's question: *"Is there anything too hard for Me?"* The answer is still "No."

Your impossibility is simply His opportunity to display glory.

Nothing Too Hard

By Edward O. Anderson, Jr.
(Inspired by Jeremiah 32:27)

When doubts arise and hope grows thin,
Lord, speak Your power deep within.
No mountain stands too tall, too wide,
When You, O God, are on my side.

You part the seas, You break the chains,
You heal the heart that fear constrains.
Remind my soul, both near and far—
There's nothing, Lord, that's too hard.

Daily Reflection:
Trusting the God of the Impossible

Promise Text: "Is there any thing too hard for Me?" — Jeremiah 32:27

1.What situation in my life feels impossible right now—and how might God be asking me to trust Him with it? (Faith begins where human strength ends.)

2. When has God surprised me by turning an impossible moment into a miracle? (Gratitude strengthens belief.)

3. How can I replace fear with faith today, declaring that nothing is too hard for God? (Speak His power louder than your problem.)

Write your answers above or in a separate journal and date it with today's date. Now give and leave it with the Lord.

When You're Waiting for Breakthrough

Waiting is not wasted time; it's sacred space where faith matures. God's delays are not denials — they are divine preparations for the joy that's coming.

Day 36 - New Mercies Every Morning

"It is of the Lord's mercies that we are not consumed,
because His compassions fail not.
They are new every morning:
great is Thy faithfulness."
— Lamentations 3:22–23

The book of Lamentations was written in the midst of destruction and despair. Jerusalem had fallen, the people were scattered, and Jeremiah wept over a nation in ruins. Yet in the middle of the ashes, he lifted his eyes and declared one of the most hopeful truths in Scripture: *"His mercies are new every morning."*

God's mercy is not rationed by the day or limited by our failures. It renews like sunrise—fresh, faithful, and unending. No matter what yesterday brought, God's compassion greets us with the dawn, reminding us that we are never too far gone for His grace to reach us.

A modern example of this truth is John Newton, the former slave trader who became a Christian pastor and wrote the timeless hymn *"Amazing Grace."* Newton's early life was filled with moral darkness and cruelty, but after surviving a violent storm at sea, he turned to God in repentance. The transformation was slow, but real—his hardened heart was reshaped by divine mercy.

In later years, he reflected, *"I am not the man I ought to be... but by the grace of God, I am what I am."* Newton's story is living proof that God's mercies can rewrite any life, no matter how broken. Every morning of his redeemed years was a testimony to the unending compassion of the Lord.

Each sunrise is an invitation to begin again.

No matter how heavy yesterday was, today comes wrapped in new mercy, new strength, and new grace.

God's faithfulness never expires—it simply renews.

New Every Morning

By Edward O. Anderson, Jr.
(Inspired by Lamentations 3:22–23)

Your mercies, Lord, each day renew,
When life feels old, You make it new.
Though I may fail, Your grace remains,
A steady love that breaks my chains.

Each dawn reminds my heart to see,
Your faithfulness surrounding me.
Through storm or sun, through joy or pain,
Your mercy sings—again, again.

Daily Reflection:
Morning Mercies

Promise Text: "They are new every morning: great is Thy faithfulness." — Lamentations 3:23

1. What part of my life today needs to experience God's new mercy the most? (Invite Him to renew what feels weary or lost.)

2. When has God's faithfulness carried me through a season when I thought I wouldn't make it? (Remembering past mercies strengthens present faith.)

3. How can I live today with gratitude for God's daily compassion, instead of guilt over yesterday's mistakes? (Mercy means you get to start again—with Him.)

Write your answers above or in a separate journal and date it with today's date. Now give and leave it with the Lord.

Day 37 - Resting While God Works

"Rest in the Lord, and wait patiently for Him:
fret not thyself because of him who prospereth in his way."
— Psalm 37:7

When life feels unfair or when others seem to move ahead while you struggle, David's words offer timeless wisdom—rest in the Lord. Rest is not inactivity; it's inner stillness that comes from trusting God's timing. Waiting on God isn't wasted time—it's sacred space where faith matures, perspective shifts, and strength is renewed. The temptation to compare or complain can steal peace, but patience allows God to finish His perfect work.

True rest is knowing that God's delay is not His denial—it's preparation for something greater than you can yet see.

A profound example of Psalm 37:7 is found in Oskar Schindler, the German businessman who risked everything to save more than 1,200 Jews during the Holocaust. At first, Schindler sought profit in wartime, but as he witnessed the brutality around him, something shifted deep within his heart. With quiet courage and patient resolve, he used his resources, influence, and even deception to shield innocent lives from certain death.

Every day, he walked the line between discovery and destruction, trusting that somehow good would triumph over evil. When the war finally ended, Schindler stood bankrupt but rich in humanity—having saved generations of families. His story embodies the heart of Psalm 37:7: to rest in God's unseen justice, to wait without despair, and to trust that righteousness will prevail in the end. Schindler's patient courage reminds us that sometimes the greatest acts of faith are done quietly, not in comfort, but in costly obedience to the whisper of God's mercy.

When impatience whispers that God has forgotten you, remember Schindler's example—and David's promise. The One you wait for is already at work. Rest doesn't mean nothing is happening; it means everything is happening according to His plan.

Resting in His Time

By Edward O. Anderson, Jr.
(Inspired by Psalm 37:7)

Lord, still my soul when storms arise,
Teach me to wait with faith-filled eyes.
While others rush, I'll rest in You,
For all You've planned will soon come true.

When fear would push or pride demand,
I'll trust Your heart, not my own hand.
In patient peace, my soul shall stay,
Until Your dawn breaks through the gray.

Daily Reflection:
Waiting Without Worry

Promise Text: "Rest in the Lord, and wait patiently for Him." — Psalm 37:7

1. What situation right now is testing my patience or tempting me to take control instead of trusting God's timing? (Surrender replaces striving.)

2. How has God proven in the past that His timing was perfect, even when I didn't understand it? (Remembering past faithfulness brings peace to present waiting.)

3. What practical way can I "rest in the Lord" today—through prayer, worship, journaling, or simply stillness? (Stillness invites God to move on your behalf.)

Write your answers above or in a separate journal and date it with today's date. Now give and leave it with the Lord.

Day 38 - Don't Give Up Before the Harvest

"And let us not be weary in well doing:
for in due season we shall reap, if we faint not."
— *Galatians 6:9*

Faithfulness often feels harder than failure because it demands endurance when results aren't visible.

Paul's encouragement to the Galatians speaks to every weary soul who has prayed, served, or sown seeds without seeing fruit. God's promises may take time, but they never expire. The waiting season is not wasted—it's the growing season. The harvest always comes in due season, not necessarily your season.

The key is not speed, but steadfastness. When you feel tempted to give up, remember that God never wastes a faithful effort, even when others don't notice.

An extraordinary modern example is Thomas Edison, who faced more than 1,000 failed attempts before inventing the practical light bulb. When asked about his failures, Edison replied, *"I have not failed. I've just found 10,000 ways that won't work."* His persistence transformed darkness into light for the world.

While Edison's success was scientific, his determination embodies a spiritual principle—don't give up when it gets hard. The moment you feel like quitting might be the moment right before your breakthrough.

God blesses the steadfast heart that keeps sowing when it's tired, trusting that the harvest is certain because the Harvester is faithful.

So, keep going. Keep praying. Keep sowing goodness into your family, ministry, or calling.

You may not see it yet, but your due season is on the way—and the Lord of the harvest never forgets a single seed.

Strength to Keep Sowing

By Edward O. Anderson, Jr.
(Inspired by Galatians 6:9)

Lord, when I'm weary, make me strong,
To keep on sowing all day long.
Though results may hide from view,
I'll trust the harvest comes from You.

Give me faith to plant again,
Though tears may fall or hearts may bend.
In due time, joy will overflow—
The seeds of love You help me sow.

Daily Reflection:
Persevering Through Weariness

Promise Text: "In due season we shall reap, if we faint not." — Galatians 6:9

1. Where in my life do I feel weary or ready to give up on something good God has called me to do? (Name the area where perseverance is needed most.)

2. What "seeds" have I planted—acts of kindness, faith, or obedience—that I need to trust God to grow in His time? (Faith sows today what it will celebrate tomorrow.)

3. How can I renew my strength today through prayer, rest, or gratitude so I don't faint in well doing? (Spiritual rest restores spiritual endurance.)

Write your answers above or in a separate journal and date it with today's date. Now give and leave it with the Lord.

Day 39 - The God Who Works All Things Together

"And we know that all things work together for good to them that love God, to them who are the called according to His purpose."
— Romans 8:28

This verse is one of the most comforting—and often misunderstood—promises in Scripture. Paul doesn't say all things are good; he says all things work together for good. Even pain, loss, and failure can become ingredients in God's greater plan.

Like a master weaver, God intertwines the dark threads and bright threads of our lives into a design more beautiful than we could imagine. When you can't see the pattern, trust the weaver. Every disappointment, delay, and detour has divine purpose when surrendered to Him.

A powerful illustration of Romans 8:28 can be seen in the life of Michael Jordan, one of the greatest athletes in history.

Before becoming a six-time NBA champion, Jordan was famously cut from his high school varsity basketball team. What could have been a moment of defeat became the catalyst for destiny. Jordan turned his disappointment into determination, later saying, *"I've failed over and over and over again in my life, and that is why I succeed."* Through every setback—injuries, losses, even the death of his father—he learned to turn pain into purpose. Jordan's journey reminds us that God can use life's rejections and failures to prepare us for greater victories.

What feels like a detour in the moment often becomes the very road God uses to fulfill His purpose and prove that all things, even the painful ones, truly work together for good.

When your heart breaks or life falls apart, remember—God's hands are still holding the pieces. What feels like an ending may be the foundation for something miraculous. Trust that He's not done writing your story, and one day, the "why" will make sense in the light of His perfect plan.

All Things for Good

Edward O. Anderson, Jr.
(Inspired by Romans 8:28)

When life feels torn and dreams are gone,
Lord, teach my heart to carry on.
Though pain may cloud what I can see,
You're working good inside of me.

The pieces fall, yet You still weave,
A masterpiece I can't conceive.
So help me trust Your sovereign hand—
All things for good, as You have planned.

Daily Reflection:
Trusting the Weaver

Promise Text: "All things work together for good to them that love God."
— Romans 8:28

1. What recent struggle or setback could God be using to shape my character or redirect my path? (Even pain has purpose in His plan.)

2. When has God taken something painful in my past and turned it into unexpected good? (Remembering past redemption strengthens faith for today.)

3. How can I show trust today—through prayer, patience, or praise—while God works behind the scenes? (Faith acts on what it believes, not just what it sees.)

Write your answers above or in a separate journal and date it with today's date. Now give and leave it with the Lord.

Day 40 - When God Wipes Every Tear

"And God shall wipe away all tears from their eyes;
and there shall be no more death, neither sorrow, nor crying,
neither shall there be any more pain: for the former things are passed away."
— Revelation 21:4

This verse is the heart's anchor for every believer who has walked through loss, pain, or despair. John's vision of the new heaven and new earth reminds us that suffering is temporary, but God's restoration is eternal. The tears we shed today are not wasted—they are noticed, recorded, and one day, wiped away by the very hand of God.

This is not a poetic promise; it's a personal one. The same Savior who wept at Lazarus's tomb will one day remove every trace of sorrow from our hearts. The pain of the present will give way to the peace of eternity.

A modern echo of hope can be found in the story of Céline Dion, the world-renowned singer who faced immense loss after the death of her husband, René Angélil, in 2016, and later, her struggles with a rare neurological condition that silenced her voice.

Despite heartbreak and illness, Céline has often spoken about finding strength through faith, love, and the belief that she will see her husband again. She said, *"You can't stop living; you have to keep going."* Her endurance through grief mirrors the truth of Revelation 21:4—pain does not have the final word.

For every tear, God promises comfort; for every loss, resurrection; for every goodbye, a coming reunion.

Even when life breaks your heart, eternity promises healing. There is coming a day when every wound will be mended, every question answered, and every tear turned to joy.

Until then, hold fast to the God who counts your tears—and prepares to wipe them away forever.

The Last Tear

By Edward O. Anderson, Jr.
(Inspired by Revelation 21:4)

Lord, when my heart is torn by pain,
Remind me loss will not remain.
For every tear Your hand will dry,
And joy will bloom where sorrows die.

You promise peace no grief can steal,
A love no wound can ever seal.
Until that day when all is new,
I'll trust Your heart to carry through.

Daily Reflection:
Holding Hope Through Tears

Promise Text: "God shall wipe away all tears from their eyes." — Revelation 21:4

1. What pain or loss in my life do I need to surrender to God's healing promise today? (Even tears can become prayers when given to Him.)

2. How can I live with eternal perspective—focusing on the coming joy instead of the present sorrow? (Hope grows when heaven feels near.)

3. Who around me needs comfort or hope today that I can share from my own journey through pain? (God often uses healed hearts to help others heal.)

Write your answers above or in a separate journal and date it with today's date. Now give and leave it with the Lord.

Afterword: When the Storm Passes

Storms never last forever. They test our faith, strip away our illusions of control, and reveal the foundation beneath our feet. Yet when the winds calm and the clouds begin to part, something remains—an unshakable reminder that God was with us through it all.

I'll never forget the typhoon that struck Manila in 1978 when I was just a preteen. My mother was in medical school at Philippine Union College and we lived in a two story house down a road that overlooked a swamp. It was one of the worst storms to ever hit the Philippines. The rain pounded so hard it felt like the sky itself was falling. The power went out, the winds howled like a living force, and before long our home was flooded with three feet of water. I remember looking down and realizing our furniture was floating. My family and I did the only thing we could—we laughed, grabbed our fishing poles, and went fishing in our own living room.

It sounds humorous now, but in that chaos, I learned one of life's greatest truths: sometimes joy and peace are choices, not conditions. Even when everything around you feels out of control, you can still find God in the moment. We didn't have light, we didn't have dry ground, but we had each other—and we had a quiet confidence that the storm would pass. And it did.

It took weeks for the water to finally dry up - I'm not sure but as I reflect on tha incident I'm almost certain it was 40 days!

That childhood storm taught me something I've carried into every season since: God does not always remove the storm, but He will always remain in it. The presence of water in the living room didn't mean God had left—it meant He was teaching us how to float....and how to fish!

If you've read this far, it means you've survived storms of your own. Maybe you've faced loss, betrayal, sickness, or despair. But if you're holding this book now, you made it. And that means the storm did not win. You are proof that faith outlasts fear.

When the next storm comes—and it will—remember this:

• Hold your peace. God is still good.
• Lift your eyes. The dawn is closer than you think.
• Trust His timing. Every storm has an expiration date.

And when the skies finally clear, may your heart whisper these words:

"Surely the Lord was in this place, and I knew it not."
— Genesis 28:16

Thank you for journeying through this storm with me. My prayer is that the same God who calmed the seas in Galilee—and a flooded house in Manila—will calm your heart, renew your strength, and fill your soul with unshakable hope.

Pastor Ed Anderson
Senior Pastor
Future of Hope Ministries

Index of Names & Stories

Adm. James Stockdale	Military / Navy POW	Integrity and endurance in suffering and captivity	85
Harriet Tubman	Abolition / Humanitarian	Courageous faith and obedience in leading others to freedom	89
Louis Zamporini	Military / Athletics	Survival, redemption, and forgiveness after unimaginable suffering	93
Kurt Warner	Sports / NFL Football	Perseverance and faith through setbacks to victory	99
Walt Disney	Entertainment / Business	Vision, creativity, and never giving up on a dream	103
Johnny Cash	Music / Faith	Redemption and grace through brokenness and renewal	107
Maya Angelou	Literature / Civil Rights	Turning pain into purpose through words and resilience	111
Serena Williams	Sports / Tennis	Strength, comeback, and perseverance through trials	115
Colonel Gail Halvorsen	Military / Air Force	Compassion and kindness during crisis ("Candy Bomber")	121
Harriet Stowe	Literature / Abolition	Using words to challenge injustice and inspire moral courage	125
Joni Eareckson-Tada	Faith / Disability Advocacy	Finding strength, purpose, and joy through suffering	129
Viktor Frankl	Psychology / Holocaust Survivor	Finding meaning in suffering through faith and purpose	133
Simone Biles	Sports / Gymnastics	Courage to rest, heal, and rise again stronger	137

Adm. William McRaven	Military / Leadership	Discipline, faith, and courage in leadership and hardship	143
Mother Teresa	Faith / Humanitarian	Compassion and God's presence in the midst of suffering	147
Desmond Doss	Military / Faith	Standing for conviction and courage under fire without violence	151
Billy Graham	Ministry / Evangelism	Unshakable faith and trust in God's love through every season	155
Rosa Parks	Civil Rights / Activism	Quiet courage that sparked a movement for justice	159
Dietrich Bonhoeffer	Theology / Resistance	Faithfulness to truth in the face of tyranny	165
Capt. Eddie Rickenbacker	Military / Aviation	Faith and survival through impossible circumstances	169
Malala Yousafzai	Education / Human Rights	Courageous faith and resilience against oppression	173
Oprah Winfrey	Media / Business	Overcoming adversity through purpose, perseverance, and grace	177
Elon Musk	Technology / Business	Persistence and innovation in the face of repeated failure	181
John Newton	Ministry / Hymn Writing	Redemption and transformation through God's amazing grace	187
Oskar Schindler	Business / Humanitarian	Courage to risk everything to save others from death	191
Thomas Edison	Science / Invention	Perseverance and vision through repeated failure	195

| Michael Jordan | Sports / Basketball | Turning rejection into motivation and victory through perseverance | 199 |
| Celine Dion | Music / Entertainment | Enduring love, loss, and recovery through faith and resilience | 203 |

Top 40 Powerful "While in the Storm" Bible Texts of Hope

Chosen for seasons of testing, pain, or uncertainty. Each verse brings a unique layer of comfort, endurance, and spiritual perspective.

When Fear Surrounds You
1. **Isaiah 43:2** – "When you pass through the waters, I will be with you; and through the rivers, they shall not overflow you."
2. **Psalm 46:1–2** – "God is our refuge and strength, a very present help in trouble. Therefore will not we fear…"
3. **Mark 4:39** – "And He arose, and rebuked the wind, and said unto the sea, Peace, be still."
4. **Psalm 91:4** – "He shall cover thee with His feathers, and under His wings shalt thou trust."
5. **John 14:27** – "Peace I leave with you, My peace I give unto you… Let not your heart be troubled, neither let it be afraid."

When You Feel Weak or Overwhelmed
6. **2 Corinthians 12:9** – "My grace is sufficient for thee: for My strength is made perfect in weakness."
7. **Philippians 4:13** – "I can do all things through Christ which strengtheneth me."
8. **Isaiah 40:31** – "But they that wait upon the Lord shall renew their strength; they shall mount up with wings as eagles."
9. **Psalm 34:18** – "The Lord is nigh unto them that are of a broken heart."
10. **Habakkuk 3:19** – "The Lord God is my strength, and He will make my feet like hinds' feet."

When Anxiety or Worry Rises
11. **1 Peter 5:7** – "Casting all your care upon Him; for He careth for you."
12. **Philippians 4:6–7** – "Be careful for nothing… and the peace of God, which passeth all understanding, shall keep your hearts and minds."
13. **Matthew 6:34** – "Take therefore no thought for the morrow."
14. **Psalm 55:22** – "Cast thy burden upon the Lord, and He shall sustain thee."
15. **Isaiah 26:3** – "Thou wilt keep him in perfect peace, whose mind is stayed on Thee."

When Darkness Seems Endless

16. **Psalm 30:5** – "Weeping may endure for a night, but joy cometh in the morning."
17. **Micah 7:8** – "When I sit in darkness, the Lord shall be a light unto me."
18. **Psalm 18:28** – "For Thou wilt light my candle: the Lord my God will enlighten my darkness."
19. **John 1:5** – "And the light shineth in darkness; and the darkness comprehended it not."
20. **Romans 8:18** – "The sufferings of this present time are not worthy to be compared with the glory which shall be revealed."

When You Need Faith to Keep Going

21. **Hebrews 11:1** – "Now faith is the substance of things hoped for, the evidence of things not seen."
22. **2 Corinthians 5:7** – "For we walk by faith, not by sight."
23. **James 1:2–4** – "Count it all joy when ye fall into divers temptations… knowing this, that the trying of your faith worketh patience."
24. **Romans 5:3–5** – "We glory in tribulations also: knowing that tribulation worketh patience."
25. **Psalm 27:13–14** – "I had fainted, unless I had believed to see the goodness of the Lord in the land of the living."

When You Feel Alone

26. **Deuteronomy 31:8** – "He will not fail thee, neither forsake thee: fear not, neither be dismayed."
27. **Matthew 28:20** – "Lo, I am with you always, even unto the end of the world."
28. **Psalm 139:7–10** – "Whither shall I go from Thy Spirit? … If I take the wings of the morning… even there shall Thy hand lead me."
29. **Romans 8:38–39** – "Nothing shall be able to separate us from the love of God."
30. **Joshua 1:9** – "Be strong and of a good courage… for the Lord thy God is with thee whithersoever thou goest."

When You Need to Remember God's Power

31. **Exodus 14:14** – "The Lord shall fight for you, and ye shall hold your peace."
32. **Psalm 107:29** – "He maketh the storm a calm, so that the waves thereof are still."
33. **Nahum 1:7** – "The Lord is good, a stronghold in the day of trouble."

34. **Ephesians 3:20** – "Now unto Him that is able to do exceeding abundantly above all that we ask or think."
35. **Jeremiah 32:27** – "Behold, I am the Lord, the God of all flesh: is there any thing too hard for Me?"

When You're Waiting for Breakthrough
36. **Lamentations 3:22–23** – "It is of the Lord's mercies that we are not consumed… great is Thy faithfulness."
37. **Psalm 37:7** – "Rest in the Lord, and wait patiently for Him."
38. **Galatians 6:9** – "And let us not be weary in well doing: for in due season we shall reap, if we faint not."
39. **Romans 8:28** – "All things work together for good to them that love God."
40. **Revelation 21:4** – "And God shall wipe away all tears from their eyes; and there shall be no more death, neither sorrow, nor crying."

Reflection
Every one of these texts is a lifeline in the storm. Together, they form a spiritual compass — guiding you to peace when life feels out of control. When you can't see the shore, let these verses remind you: The storm doesn't have the final word — the Savior does.

Bonus Texts

When Dealing with Anger
1. **Ephesians 4:26–27** – "Be angry, and do not sin; do not let the sun go down on your wrath, nor give place to the devil."
2. **James 1:19–20** – "Let every person be quick to hear, slow to speak, slow to anger; for the anger of man does not produce the righteousness of God."
3. **Proverbs 15:1** – "A soft answer turns away wrath, but a harsh word stirs up anger."
4. **Proverbs 29:11** – "A fool gives full vent to his spirit, but a wise man quietly holds it back."
5. **Colossians 3:8** – "But now you must put them all away: anger, wrath, malice, slander, and obscene talk from your mouth."

When Facing Frustration
1. **Psalm 37:7** – "Be still before the Lord and wait patiently for him; do not fret when people succeed in their ways."

2. **Philippians 4:6–7** – "Do not be anxious about anything, but in every situation, by prayer and petition, with thanksgiving, present your requests to God."
3. **Isaiah 40:31** – "But those who wait for the Lord shall renew their strength; they shall mount up with wings like eagles."
4. **Galatians 6:9** – "And let us not grow weary of doing good, for in due season we will reap, if we do not give up."
5. **Psalm 46:10** – "Be still, and know that I am God."

When Disappointed
1. **Romans 8:28** – "And we know that all things work together for good to those who love God, to those who are called according to His purpose."
2. **Psalm 34:18** – "The Lord is near to the brokenhearted and saves the crushed in spirit."
3. **Proverbs 3:5–6** – "Trust in the Lord with all your heart, and lean not on your own understanding."
4. **Lamentations 3:22–23** – "Because of the Lord's great love we are not consumed… His mercies are new every morning."
5. **John 16:33** – "In this world you will have trouble. But take heart! I have overcome the world."

When Searching for Purpose
1. **Jeremiah 29:11** – "For I know the plans I have for you, declares the Lord… plans to give you hope and a future."
2. **Romans 12:2** – "Do not be conformed to this world, but be transformed by the renewal of your mind… that you may discern the will of God."
3. **Ephesians 2:10** – "For we are His workmanship, created in Christ Jesus for good works, which God prepared beforehand."
4. **Proverbs 19:21** – "Many are the plans in a person's heart, but it is the Lord's purpose that prevails."
5. **Micah 6:8** – "He has shown you, O man, what is good; and what does the Lord require of you but to do justice, to love mercy, and to walk humbly with your God."

"Anger tests your control, frustration tests your patience, disappointment tests your faith—but purpose redeems them all. When you know why God placed you here, what once provoked you will no longer move you, because your peace is anchored to His plan, not your pain."
- Pastor Ed Anderson

About the Author

Pastor Ed Anderson was born in Inglewood, California—right in the middle of the Watts riots. From his first breath, life seemed determined to teach him how to stand strong when the world shakes. And shake it did. He grew up through some of the most powerful earthquakes to rock Southern California, where the ground wasn't the only thing that moved—you had to keep your faith steady, too.

As a pre-teen, Ed lived overseas in the Philippines, learning how to survive both typhoons and martial law. When one of the worst storms in 1978 flooded his family's Manila home with three feet of water, young Ed did what any resilient kid would do—he went fishing in the living room. That moment became a lifelong picture of joy in chaos and humor under pressure.

Later, back in the U.S., he grew up in *Tortilla Flats*—a lively stretch of Torrance, California, where neighbors were colorful, gangs ruled the streets, and every day felt like a test of faith and reflexes. "If you could dodge bullets," he laughs, "you could probably dodge most of life's problems." Those years on the gritty streets of Los Angeles taught him resilience, perseverance, and a grounded faith that would later define his ministry.

That same street-smart toughness carried into adulthood, where Pastor Ed would go on to serve in over 40 national and international disaster responses, including the World Trade Center attacks on 9/11, Hurricane Katrina, and

216

numerous humanitarian crises around the world such as the Indonesia floods and Tsunami.

Whether digging through rubble, comforting the grieving, or preaching hope in refugee camps, Ed learned that storms come in many forms—but faith, compassion, and courage are the only shelters that never fail.

Today, he serves as Senior Pastor of a thriving Church in Arizona and leads Future of Hope Ministries, reaching millions worldwide through preaching, media, music, and international evangelism.

He has seen God move in the calm and in the chaos—from the streets of Los Angeles to the flooded homes of Manila, from Ground Zero to the mission fields of the Philippines, Russia, Cambodia, Chile, and Micronesia.

When he's not writing or preaching, you'll find Ed composing songs, leading mission teams, or telling stories that somehow mix laughter, tears, and faith into one message: No matter how fierce the storm, God is still in control—and He's still in the boat with you.

Future of Hope Ministries

Bringing Light to a World in Crisis

Every storm has a story—and every story needs hope.

Future of Hope Ministries exists to share the gospel of Jesus Christ through preaching, digital media, music, and global mission projects that reach hearts across every nation.

From disaster zones to digital platforms, from mountain villages to city streets, our mission is simple: To reveal God's love, restore faith, and raise a generation ready for Jesus' soon return.

What We Do

• **Evangelistic Campaigns:** Global and local outreach across the U.S., Philippines, Chile, Kenya, and beyond.

• **Media & Broadcasting:** The Future of Hope YouTube channel, reaching millions with messages of faith, prophecy, and redemption.

• **Books & Devotionals:** Powerful resources like *While in the Storm* and *365 Days of Hope*, designed to encourage and equip believers.

• **Music & Worship Projects:** Inspiring songs and albums through Future of Hope Music and SkyWalk Records.

• **Disaster Response & Humanitarian Work:** Bringing help and healing to those impacted by crisis through faith-based partnerships and relief efforts.

Contact & Connection
Future of Hope Ministries
19445 W. Indian School Road, Ste. 102-304
Litchfield Park, AZ 85340
info@futureofhope.com
www.FutureofHope.com

YouTube: @FutureofHope
Instagram | Facebook | TikTok: @FutureofHopeMinistries

Partner With Us

Every view, prayer, and gift fuels the mission of hope.

When you support Future of Hope Ministries, you help send the gospel to unreached regions, build schools and churches, feed the hungry, and bring light to places of darkness.

Join the movement.

Together, let's bring the world a Future of Hope.

Future of Hope Website
www.FutureofHope.com

Future of Hope YouTube Channel
YouTube.com/@FutureOfHope

Partner With Us

Be Part of the Movement.

Share the Message. Bring Hope to the World.

Every storm someone survives has a story of grace behind it—and every story of grace begins with someone who cared enough to help.

Your prayers, partnership, and generosity allow Future of Hope Ministries to reach souls through preaching, books, digital evangelism, and life-changing mission projects around the world.

Together, we are building a movement of faith that declares:

"Even in the storm, there is hope."

Ways Your Partnership Makes a Difference
• Funds evangelistic campaigns across Asia, Africa, and the Americas.
• Produces life-transforming media and broadcasts that reach millions.
• Supports local churches, schools, and humanitarian relief projects.
• Provides Bibles, books, and discipleship tools for new believers.
• Trains and equips pastors, youth leaders, and mission volunteers.

Partnership Levels

Hope Supporter – Monthly gifts up to $25
Help share messages of hope through online media, devotionals, and Bible study resources that reach new audiences every day.

Hope Builder – Monthly gifts of $26–$99
Empower gospel campaigns, fund the printing of evangelistic materials, and provide on-the-ground support for mission teams and follow-up ministries.

Hope Ambassador – Monthly gifts of $100 or more
Fuel major mission projects—church planting, humanitarian relief, and large-scale global evangelism. As a Hope Ambassador, you help light entire nations with the gospel.

How to Give

Give securely online at www.FutureofHope.com
or mail your tax-deductible gift to:

Future of Hope Ministries
19445 W. Indian School Road, Ste. 102-304
Litchfield Park, AZ 85340
info@futureofhope.com

Thank You

Because of your partnership, countless lives have already been changed—
and many more will be. Every gift, large or small, becomes a lifeline of faith
for someone walking through their own storm.

Together, we are bringing the world a Future of Hope.

"The light shines in the darkness, and the darkness has not overcome it."
— John 1:5

Other Books by the Author

The Sabbath Revolution Series (Coming Soon)
A groundbreaking multi-volume series uncovering the forgotten power of the Sabbath as God's ultimate gift of rest, renewal, and resistance in an age of chaos. This series will reveal how Sabbath was not just a command—but a revolution of grace, freedom, and restoration for humanity. From Eden to eternity, *The Sabbath Revolution* Series invites readers to rediscover the rhythm that realigns the soul with the Creator.

The Rhythm of God (Coming Soon)
The first volume in *The Sabbath Revolution* Series, this beautifully written work explores how God built rhythm into creation, faith, and everyday life. Through poetic reflection and deep biblical insight, Pastor Ed shows how Sabbath is not just a day—it's a heartbeat that restores balance, joy, and divine purpose. A perfect book for those longing to slow down, breathe again, and find spiritual harmony in a hurried world.

Wisdom from a Father - 2nd Edition (Coming Soon)
Inspiring and powerful true stories of wisdom and life lessons about Pastor Ed Anderson's father, Edward O. Anderson, Sr. In this touching collection of short stories, Pastor Ed reflects on the lessons, laughter, and legacy of a father who taught faith through everyday life. From moments of humor to quiet strength to hard discipline, these stories capture the essence of godly fatherhood and remind every reader that wisdom often comes through the ordinary moments we share—and the people who shape us most.

While in the Storm (You're holding it now!)
A moving, faith-filled exploration of how God's presence sustains us through life's fiercest trials. Drawing from personal experience—including surviving the 1978 Manila typhoon, major earthquakes, and global disaster responses—Pastor Ed reveals that even when everything seems out of control, God is never absent.

Countdown to Eternity: Prophecy Quick-Start Guide (Coming Soon)
A clear, engaging introduction to end-time prophecy and hope. Written for a new generation of seekers, this book reveals how ancient symbols and modern events connect to God's final call of love and redemption.

Stories I Wish I Heard at 15 (Coming Soon)
True and fictionalized stories of wisdom, pain, and growth—told with cinematic emotion and spiritual insight. Each short story ends with a life reflection, speaking to young hearts searching for identity, purpose, and grace.

And Many More Coming Soon

Stay connected for upcoming releases by Pastor Ed Anderson including:
• 365 Days of Hope: A Guide to Strength and Encouragement
• Courage Under Command: Faith and Firearms in the Service of God
• Seize the Moment: Unleashing the Power of Proactivity and Decisive Action
• Heartwork: 10 Days to a Transformed Life
• After the Storm: Life After the End of the World
• Aloha Iesu: Songs and Devotions from the Islands (Music Series)
• Bible Screen Watch: Christian Reviews of Streaming Shows
• She Was Brave: 7 Women Who Changed History with Courage
• The Doctrine of Self-Defense
• The Great Week of Time
• The Rising Storm
• Voices of Every Nation
• 365 Days of Wonder

To learn more about Pastor Ed Anderson's books, devotionals, and global ministry work, visit:
www.FutureofHope.com/books
info@futureofhope.com